Voices from the Camps

A People's History of Palestinian Refugees in Jordan, 2006

Nabil Marshood

UNIVERSITY PRESS OF AMERICA,® INC.

Lanham • Boulder • New York • Toronto • Plymouth, UK

Copyright © 2010 by
University Press of America,® Inc.
4501 Forbes Boulevard
Suite 200
Lanham, Maryland 20706
UPA Acquisitions Department (301) 459-3366

Estover Road
Plymouth PL6 7PY
United Kingdom

Library of Congress Control Number: 2009943408
ISBN: 978-0-7618-5047-2 (paperback : alk. paper)
eISBN: 978-0-7618-5048-9

In memory of my parents

The writer's function is not without arduous duties. By definition, he cannot serve today those who make history; he must serve those who are subject to it.

—Albert Camus

Contents

PART III: VOICES FROM THE CAMPS

Illustrations

Preface

My roots go back to a small Palestinian village of Al-Mazra'a in Israel. *Al-Mazra'a* is Arabic for "the farm," which denotes the cultural and economic structure of the community. Put in the American context, *Al-Mazra'a* would be referred to as Mazra'aville. Growing up, I heard stories of displacement and loss. A large number of Palestinians, including one of my aunts and a number of my father's cousins, had become refugees, scattered in camps sponsored by the United Nations in the surrounding countries: Lebanon and Syria to the north; Jordan to the east; and Egypt to the south. One of my uncles had disappeared on his way to work one day, never to return home, leaving behind his wife and two little daughters. The ugly violent face of the war of 1948 had taken away his life. Years later, despite the passage of time, my elderly grandmother would cross the citrus field separating our homes and ask me to write letters to the Israeli authorities and to a special radio program designed for the purpose of seeking and searching for missing persons. My grandmother refused to accept her son's disappearance, hoping her letters would bring answers. As I sat and wrote, she and my mother would pour out their feelings of loss and of hope.

The tragedy was profound. It was a trauma that the Palestinian people had not experienced before. Nations and conquerors had come and gone; but, forcing the Palestinian people out of their homes and preventing them from returning to their homes was an intense traumatic experience of personal, national and cultural dimensions. The community had collapsed, and Palestine as they had known it was no longer there. No wonder Palestinians call it *Al-Nakba* ("The Catastrophe"). Some were angry, many were confused, others were in denial; and all were sad and frightened. Not much was left for them. Having lost their family members, their land, their homes, and their basic elements of survival, Palestinians had become refugees by imposition. Their social position was transformed from land owners with a culture rooted in the land to laborers and refugees—an "imposed status" that is neither achieved nor ascribed. Thus, Palestinians found themselves defending their right to exist as a people and as a community.

Existential struggles leave a mark on those affected by them. Had Palestinians lost their identity? Had they lost their dignity? Was there any hope left for them? Who was responsible for such tragedy? If God were good, why would He allow such tragedy to happen? I recall my mother asking repeatedly, "Why do bad things happen to good people?" The questions were endless.

The sixties were formative years for me. As a young teenager, I was an Israeli citizen with a growing list of questions. Endowed with the history of the Palestinian trauma, I realized that the Jewish people had recently suffered a trauma of their own, the Holocaust; and that Britain had promised the Jewish people a homeland in Palestine under the auspices of the Balfour Declaration. These facts made matters even more complicated. Now my query expanded: Why did Britain give away a land which they never possessed? Who gave Britain the right to do so? Why would the Jewish people act aggressively toward the Palestinians?—The Jewish and Palestinian people had lived in this land for centuries and in many ways had shared a common culture. What had made the difference? Why couldn't Palestinians and Jews live together and share the land? The war of 1948 had ended, so why were the Palestinians denied their right to return to their homes? Why did the Holocaust take place? Should Palestinians be held responsible for the atrocities of the Holocaust?

My questions were numerous, but the answers were nowhere to be found. I had witnessed violence, wars, and conflict, and I was scared. I saw how one group could easily control another. I was cynical of humanity. Thus, I concluded the reality was not good: Not only had Palestinians suffered, but also those who had resorted to violence paid a heavy price—they lost their soul.

Questions were the hallmark of an ongoing dialogue within the Palestinian community. But dialogue was all there was. Although dialogue, questions, and debate don't change reality, they are useful for cathartic purposes as a way to overcome trauma. Most importantly, they keep alive both the collective memory and the conflict. This, I reckon, was one of the forces that has reshaped the Palestinian identity and preserved it for more than sixty years now.

As my family listened to the radio in those days, I would also hear speeches by Gamal Abdel Nasser of Egypt. Nasser spoke of modernity and freedom of speech. He was passionate about it and often declared in his speeches, "Freedom of speech is the first introductory step toward democracy." His words moved me.

Listening to the debate, dialogue, and questions, I concluded that coping with this trauma required education. I came to believe in the power of the pen not of the gun. My parents, like most Palestinian parents, emphasized the value of education. I adopted this sentiment and took it one step further: Education is important, I argued, not only because of its power to transform those who possess it, but also because it has the power to transform reality. Education provides a way for one to connect with something greater than oneself. I encouraged friends and people around me to acquire an education and to educate others about their experiences. Doing so, I believed, was both empowering and enlightening. It was also democratic. Perhaps if Israel understood the reality of the Palestinians, it would change its behavior and its policy. I thought that once powerful nations understood the tragedies of both Palestinians and the Jewish people, they would come together to offer a helping hand to both. In short, I believed in the goodness in humanity. And I still do.

As a teenager, determined that education was the key to change, I declared to my mother that I want to become a college professor. With her gentle, soft and caring manners, she gave me a hug and said: "We are proud of you; you can become whatever you want to be." My father was all smiles; he couldn't hide his pride.

Now fast forward to the present: At the start of the new millennium, a new era began. The September 11, 2001 attacks on the World Trade Center and the Pentagon will be remembered as a turning point in history. They mark a moment in time that divides history into two eras: before and after 9/11. Following those attacks, I felt sad and confused. Again, the solution was education. So, now as an American and a college professor, I helped organize along with others at my home college, Hudson County Community College, in New Jersey, a vigil that brought students, faculty, administration, and the public together. I remembered my mother and grandmother's story and, in addressing the audience, wrote the following lines:

> . . . My heart goes out to the victims of the horrible attack on America and to their families. From their resting place up there in heaven, both my grandmother and mother share your pain. And as they weep with us today, they remind us of what they had taught me years ago:
>
>> Go forth now and seek love, not hatred.
>> Go forth now and seek justice, not cruelty.
>> It is only with love that you can bring life.
>> And it is only with justice that you can bring peace.

Yet conflicts have a life of their own. The events of September 11, 2001 brought about a new wave of wars in the Middle East with global repercussions of unforeseen magnitude. The United States has declared a war on terror that seems to have no end, and its domestic policy and international relations have changed. Sadly, in addition to the victims of 9/11, Americans have lost some of their civil liberties; America is at risk of losing its democratic soul, while people in the Middle East, particularly in Iraq, Afghanistan, and Palestine, are also losing their lives. The political, economic, and religious repercussions are such that a paradigm shift is now taking place, one that will have a long-lasting impact on the United States, the Middle East, and the world in general. In this new paradigm, the Palestinian cause has been placed by the United States, Israel, and many European nations, in the context of the war on terror thus redefining it and making a just cause illegitimate.

The Palestinian-Israeli conflict has also taken on a new dimension. While Israel has managed to capitalize on power, wealth and property, the Palestinian side has a different narrative: Palestinian political leaders are more divided than ever before; a large segment (15.5%) of Palestinians remain in refugee camps; Israel not only continues to occupy the West Bank and Gaza, but also has divided those territories into small isolated communities in which Palestinian residents experience violence and humiliation on a daily basis. Moreover, Israel has built a huge winding wall that separates the Palestinian from their own land and in many cases from their own families. This will also separate the Palestinian territories of the West Bank from Israel proper, reconstituting those territories into a prison-like environment. Oppression of Palestinians is now a function of internal turmoil and external forces. Yet the international community, including the United States, Europe, Israel, the Arab nations, and the Palestinian Authority, continue to talk about the "peace process." But is the process more important than the outcome? In a sociological sense, one could argue that this conflict seems to be "functional." That is to say, persistence of this conflict, not its solution, is rather useful for the existing hegemony. Not only do powerful nations such as the United States, Israel, European nations and a number of the Arab countries seem to benefit from the ongoing conflict by capitalizing on their hegemony, weapon trade, land expansion, and domination of the Arab population, but also Palestinians have become mere pawns in their hands. The tragedy is that average Palestinians are carrying the burden and the cost of an elusive peace.

Given such complexities, what does it mean to be a Palestinian in the present era? This book addresses this question from the refugees' perspective. Its theme rests on the notion that down deep at the heart of it all one finds the human, quiet voice: the voice of the oppressed. It is the voice that matters most, because it has the power to transform reality. It is the power of humanity.

Nabil Marshood
May 2009

Acknowledgments

This book is the culmination of fifty years of regular observations of the Palestinian-Israeli conflict and its impact on the Palestinians. It is also the result of more than twenty years of teaching at an urban, inner-city community college. Similarities and differences notwithstanding, I have learned much about the effects of oppression on the human character and on the life of a community as it responds to oppression. I am greatly indebted to all those who came my way and informed my intellectual and scholarly endeavors.

This work couldn't have been done without the refugees themselves. I don't believe I can thank them enough for their generosity with time and attention. This work is for them and about them. Their stories and experiences are recorded in the pages of this book so as to echo in the core of human consciousness. I will forever be indebted to them.

I thank my late parents who suffered injustice yet inspired me to pursue justice, and who taught me to care for the less fortunate in our midst.

I am deeply appreciative of the funding granted to me by the Fulbright Scholar program to pursue my research on this human tragedy. Their support is indeed recognition of the importance of my work, and is a validation of the gravity of this catastrophe as well as of the humanity of those who suffer from it. The staff at the Fulbright House in Amman, Jordan, headed by Alain McNamara, opened their doors and their hearts and made me feel at home. I am much obliged for their time, talent and contribution to my work.

My sincere thanks also to the staff of the Department of Palestinian Affairs (DPA) in Jordan, headed by Mr. Wajeeh Azayzeh, and the staff of the United Nations Relief & Work Agency (UNRWA) offices in Jordan, particularly Mr. Matar Saqr. I thank them for the time they spent with me and for providing me with relevant data, information and contacts.

The staffs at the Center for Strategic Studies (CSS) of Jordan University, headed by Dr. Mustafa Hamarneh, and at the Center for the Study of Refugees and Displaced Persons at Yarmouk University, headed by Dr. Ali Zagal, were more than helpful. I thank them for their time, guidance, knowledge and hospitality. From Jordan University, I give special thanks to Dr. Ibrahim Saif, Mr. Saleem Haddad, and Dr. Ibrahim Othman. And From Yarmouk University, my sincere thanks to Dr. Abedalbaset Athamneh, and Dr. Khalaf Taani.

I am indebted to Dr. Abegail D. Johnson of Hudson County Community College; to the Honorable Azmat Hassan, Former Ambassador of Pakistan; to the Reverend Charles Rawlings of the Presbytery of Newark; to professor Anthony Wanis St. John of American University; to professor Saliba Sarsar of Monmouth University; to Emmy Award-winning Journalist, Anisa Mehdi; to professor Barry Tomkins of Hudson County Community College; and to professor Michael Botterweck of Triton College for their support, words of encouragement, editorial advice and insightful remarks. I also thank Mr. Charles Bibbins and Mr. Ian Grodman for proofreading this manuscript.

The closeness of my extended family just across the border in Israel made the physical distance from my immediate family in the United States much easier to bear. My two visits with my brothers and sisters and their families in the Galilee, and with my in-laws in Jerusalem, gave me the warmth I needed during such a long separation. Special thanks also go to my brother Fathi for his invaluable insight and encouragement.

I thank my friends from my home state of New Jersey. The knowledge that they were there for my family during my absence, if and when needed, put my mind at ease. They are too numerous to mention by name, but they know who they are. My family and I are sincerely grateful for their friendship.

And above all, I thank my best friend and partner in life, my wife Miriam, for her love, strength, and support; and my children, Tamer and Ruba, who continue to inspire me.

Introduction

This book will take you on a journey inside a number of Palestinian refugee camps in Jordan. As on any journey, one needs to be prepared and equipped, and ready to encounter the unfamiliar and the unexpected. Along the way, I encourage you to acquire the "sociological imagination;"[1] that is, a way of thinking that suspends judgment of the prevailing notions of accepted political reality and allows the observer to view the expedition with an open mind. One is there to explore, to learn, and to make connections that are not obvious. In the pursuit of understanding refugees and their identities, personal biography is correlated with social structure. In their classic hypothesis, also known as the Thomas theorem, William I. Thomas and Dorothy S. Thomas argued, "If men define situations as real, they are real in their consequences,"[2] suggesting that human interpretations of a situation affect their action and that establishing a definition of the situation requires the participants agree on both the context—a framework of the interaction—and on their identities. For the purpose of this research, individual testimonials and personal narratives of the refugees essentially define their imposed refugee status and its associated characteristics.

As a traveler, be prepared to be enriched with new information, surprised on occasions and challenged at times. Being ready for new insights makes the journey a rewarding adventure. You may begin by looking at your personal baggage: your biases, prejudices, political agendas, attitudes, and the like. This is heavy baggage to carry on such a journey. Try to leave it behind and start afresh to learn, inquire, and examine with an open mind. Allow yourself to encounter reality, including what may seem "inconvenient truth," in the sense that the Nobel Peace Prize winner, Al Gore, uses the term.

For explorers of people's history, it is worth mentioning some important observations. Harry S. Truman had remarked that "No two historians ever agree on what happened, and the damn thing is they both think they're telling the truth." Napoleon Bonaparte had also noted that "History is a myth agreed upon." And the American Nobel Prize winner for Literature William Faulkner had asserted that "The past isn't dead; it isn't even past." The complexities imbedded in the study of history compel the explorer to sort the official history of the state or the group from the myths surrounding it. As in all narratives, personal history, which constitutes the core of people's history, may or may not coincide with the official and documented history. Nonetheless, since the state's official history is usually written by the victorious, people's history becomes an essential component in the larger enterprise of understanding human affairs. It may not be ignored for it has the power to enrich humanity with its multifaceted contributions to the understanding of existential endeavors, particularly of marginal, oppressed and invisible groups.

The purpose of this journey is to bring refugee camp life and its people much closer, so one can face—and hopefully understand—their reality as well as their humanity. As an eager traveler, one must be free to question all one sees on the road and, thus, be guided by the axiom posed by Voltaire, "Judge a man by his questions rather than by his answers."

This study is about understanding the human dimension of the plight of Palestinian refugees. It is about their human experience—the trauma and the narrative that are missing from public discourse. What does it mean to be a refugee? How have Palestinian refugees survived in a stateless condition for as long as they have? What does it mean to be a Palestinian refugee in Jordan? Do they suffer from discrimination? Do they enjoy equal rights? Do they receive equal services and opportunities? Do they perceive themselves as Palestinians or Jordanians? Do they long to return to Palestine? Will they accept another settlement? What are their dreams and aspirations? What effect have these oppressive conditions had on their aspirations, dreams and identity? The questions are numerous, but the point here is to bring to our consciousness that, despite the fact that refugees in general, and Palestinian refugees in particular, have suffered from decisions made for them and about them, they have their own views, dreams and aspirations, and wish to be part of the decisions that affect their lives.

It is questions of this nature that have the potential to shed light on the humanity of those who have become invisible and have been denied one of their most basic human rights—that of living in their own homes. The purpose of this study, then, is to explore the people's history of Palestinian refugees, the most invisible of all Palestinians, and to present their narrative of the events that have led to their current circumstances with the aim of understanding the effects of such conditions and events on their national identity.

The objectives of this study are twofold.

The first objective is to present the findings of ethnographic research based on field observation and interviews with Palestinians living in a number of refugee camps in Jordan during the period January through May 2006. This research was carried out as an exploratory, qualitative study designed to understand the social reality of Palestinian refugees from their own perspective, and to learn about the arrangements they have made for their families, their children, and their communities. In short, this study is a report of people's history and its consequences on their identity.

A second objective of this study is to advance the literature in two areas. Although the literature on the Palestinian-Israeli conflict is vast and covers a wide range of fields, sociological and psychological research on Palestinian refugees is lacking. Because traumatic experiences may shake the foundations of one's beliefs about safety and shatter his/her assumptions of trust, and because they can be so far outside what is usually expected that the reactions they provoke may appear unusual or out of the ordinary, they are often best described in the words of those who experienced them. This study is intended to contribute to the literature on refugees in general and Palestinian refugees in particular, by bringing the voice of Palestinian refugees in Jordan much closer to the reader.

This study may also contribute to the literature is bringing the sociological perspective closer to the study of refugees and "refugeehood." Despite the magnitude of the international refugees' problem, the field is left in the hand of human rights organizations, political scientists, and historians. At the same time, the humanizing disciplines, including sociology and psychology, remained on the periphery.

Thus, it is anticipated that this exploratory study will raise more questions, generate new hypotheses, and propose conceptual and theoretical frameworks, which may inspire the parties to the conflict not only to find a solution to this terrible refugee problem but also to further intellectual and scientific inquiry in this field.

Palestinian refugees are scattered in a number of refugee camps in the region.[3] Jordan has the largest number of Palestinian refugees outside the West Bank, Gaza, and Israel. Most of those refugees in Jordan, with the exception of the displaced refugees of 1967 from Gaza, were granted Jordanian citizenship. These facts pose the question as to whether citizenship status makes a difference in the identity and the aspiration of those refugees.

To be clear, this study is not about solutions, but about understanding the social reality of being a Palestinian refugee. Nevertheless it is hoped that it will inform the solution seekers. Human beings are capable of finding solutions to problems of their own making. Propositions for solutions to the

Palestinian-Israeli conflict are abundant, but not one has yet brought about a final, peaceful, and just settlement. Thus, some of the important questions raised by this conflict are: Why is it that after so many years of this ongoing conflict an equitable and just settlement has not been reached? What forces stand against a final, just and peaceful settlement? And why is it that after more than sixty years, the human community finds it acceptable to force people to reside in a refugee camp environment? Is there a political will to acknowledge and to find a solution to this tragedy? This study is not intended to address these specific questions. Yet, if human history is to be grounded in social reality, this study may shed some light on the living conditions and plight of the Palestinian refugees in Jordan that may lead to a conclusion sooner rather than later.

NOTES

1. C. Wright Mills, *Sociological Imagination* (New York: Oxford University Press, 1959).

2. William I. Thomas and Dorothy S. Thomas, *The Child in America: Behavior Problems and Programs* (New York: Knopf, 1928), 571-572.

3. UNRWA is the only agency that collects data on Palestinian refugees that fall under its jurisdiction. http://www.un.org/unrwa/publications/index.html (27 Aug. 2008).

Part One

IDENTITY AND CULTURE

Chapter One

Identity and Culture

TOWARD A THEORY OF IDENTITY: A BRIEF OUTLINE

Identity is a function of social interactions, which is to say, identity is a social and cultural construct that has a meaningful existence only in relation to others. As such it embodies the essence and core of humanity. Said differently, accepting one's total identity is in fact accepting their humanity, as well as their rights, claims and obligations. Total identity is used here to refer to the multidimensional facets of the individual and his/her complex reality which represents the personal, cultural, emotional, religious, political and national characteristics of that individual and his or her group.

The notion that identity is correlated with social interactions is important to highlight because it points to the fact that identity is not limited to self-definition, but rather it might also be influenced by definitions given by others around them. Identity therefore could be used in a number of ways by the individual and by those around him/her. It becomes a fluid concept that could be interpreted in a variety of ways depending on the historical, political, cultural or national context. I suggest that in situations in which the total identity is accepted, humanity is recognized. But in conflicting environments, humanity is suppressed. Under such oppressive conditions, identity could become narrow and incomplete, almost hollow. In situations entrenched with conflict, the parties to the conflict tend to impose a narrow, one-dimensional conception of identity onto their adversaries. Given such interactions, parties with a greater degree of power can ultimately manipulate the identity of the other. It is in such an environment that the "Other" is constructed to become the bearer of the negative, and the target of racism, and stereotypes.

Overcoming such a troubling reality becomes a challenging task. Identity, I argue, must not to be limited to the biological, tribal or social constructs.

It is also a function of our individual creation. Moreover, it is of paramount importance to point out that our understanding of humanity in general and of the Palestinian narrative in particular requires the inclusion of personal stories and the study of one's history. Such examination takes us beyond the labels, breaks down stereotypes, and enriches our understanding of human existential and spiritual struggles. It also puts forwards the notion that identity is a complex construct that might be shaped by a number of factors.

1. *Biological or tribal affiliations*—This concept refers to the notion that identity is a function of biological, racial or ethnic group affiliations. These conditions are a consequence of birth and stand beyond the control of the individual. To be clear, I use the term ethnicity as an inclusive construct that refers to cultural heritage composed of language, religion, and nationality.
2. *Relations with outsiders*—Individuals or communities who maintain close interactions with a *limited* number of external groups tend to hold onto a conservative view of the world, and are likely to be intolerant of differences and, more importantly, to isolate themselves into segregated communities and hold onto a fixed and/or rigid identity. These factors may be a function of cultural socialization or individual/cultural choice. Communities such as the Amish and the Hasidic Jews in the United States serve as examples. Communities of this type are also likely to highlight their biological or ethnic affinities.
3. *Individual choice*—These factors are typical of the modern era where individualism is the paramount characteristic of society. In this context, individuals construct their identities and make their own choices transcending cultural, tribal, racial or ethnic dimensions that were imposed on them. This is the process of remaking one's self that seems to play a major role in the formation of the modern person.

It is obvious then that identity formation is a process that continues to evolve rather than be defined by a single event or occurrence. Identity is the outcome of multidimensional frames made out of time, place and group affiliation. Histories, and individual and collective memories of the past, are as vital as a person's present outlook and future orientation. Put simply, where the individual came from in terms of time and place is as important as where he is located at present and where he is going into the future.

Another way to conceptualize the process of identity formation is to think of the act of throwing a stone into a quiet pond. This act will produce ripples, or circular waves of water. Identity formation is a function of interactions between the individual with the circles or spheres of people and communities and their cultures that exist around them. *Community spheres* refer to ethnic, religious and national communities that have the potential to shape one's identity. Identity construction begins with the immediate sphere but it might expand to include the outer circles as well. Movement from one sphere to the next will create new spheres of communities and form new opportunities.

Identity, therefore, is the result of three sets of factors that extend from those where the individual, on one end of the continuum, has the least amount of control and choice, to the other extreme where the individual has the highest level of control in reconstructing themselves. However, since individual choice does not exist in absolute terms, the social, political and cultural environment of that individual might play a major role in determining their choice. It could be argued then, that open societies offer the individual more chances and more opportunities for personal choice and for open interactions that transcend the immediate sphere of their original biological or tribal affiliations.

Community spheres are not defined by physical or geographic proximity. The notion that individuals' identities might be influenced by groups that are physically or even culturally different from their own is not a new idea. The concept of a reference group is an instrument that could facilitate such a process. Members of racial and ethnic minority groups in the United States carry hyphenated identities. Such is the case for African-Americans, Hispanic-Americans, Jewish-Americans, Muslim-Americans, Irish-Americans, Asian-Americans, Arab-Americans, Italian-Americans, and the like. Although most members of those groups have achieved a high degree of assimilation in the American society, consider themselves Americans and have made a significant contribution to the American culture, their identities are also influenced by their original ethnic or religious groups. Hyphenated identities or dual identities represent a split in the power dynamics of society, where their members are always compared with their original culture and simultaneously with their new adopted culture. Hyphenated identities exist either as a result of fear on the part of minority groups of losing their original roots in an all-open society; or because of their heightened level of ethnic pride; or, alternatively, fear on the part of the majority or dominant group about encroachment of minorities into their environment, that prompts their rejecting and segregating them.

THE QUESTION AT HAND—
UNDERSTANDING PALESTINIAN IDENTITY

The question before us relates to the Palestinian Diaspora. How do these theoretical concepts interact to construct the identity of the Palestinians in general and refugees in particular? To address this question, one must address another, more fundamental question: who is a Palestinian?

Palestinians are a people who racially belong to the Semitic tribes of the Middle East that trace their roots centuries back to the Canaanites. It was the Canaanites who, more than 6000 years ago built Jericho, one of the world's most ancient cities; it is also believed that the city of Bethlehem (in Arabic, "Beit Lahem"), was named after "The house of Lahman" (a Canaanite God).[1] There seems to be an agreement that the name *Palestine* is derived from the Greek word *Philistinoi* referring to "the people of the sea" who came from Greece and settled in the southern region of Canaan, modern Palestine/Israel, and assimilated into Canaanite culture. According to the Jewish Virtual Library, "The term "Palestine" is believed to be derived from the Philistines, an Aegean people who, in the 12th Century B.C., settled along the Mediterranean coastal plain of what is now Israel and the Gaza Strip."[2]

Historically, Palestinians pride themselves on being a "nation" built on the principles of inclusion and universality. Muslims, Christians, Druze, Jews, and Baha'i, among others, were considered Palestinians until the formation of the Jewish state that separated itself from its original body to form an independent, exclusive identity.[3] Consequently, the term *Palestinian* was reconstructed to include all of these religious groups except the Jewish people.

Keeping in mind the lack of a central data source for the Palestinians, it is generally estimated that there are about nine million Palestinians worldwide. Seventy-two percent of them (6.5 million) reside in Israel, the West Bank, Gaza and the neighboring Arab countries. It is also estimated that the total Palestinian refugee population stands at about 5 million—fifty-six percent of all Palestinians, and that about 1.4 million, constituting about 15.5% of all Palestinians, reside in refugee camps scattered in the West Bank, Gaza, Jordan, Lebanon, and Syria.[4]

United Nations Relief and Work Agency (UNRWA) was formed to serve the humanitarian needs of Palestinian refugees. According to its definition,[5] "Palestinian refugees are persons whose normal place of residence was Palestine between June 1946 and May 1948, who lost both their homes and means of livelihood as a result of the 1948 Arab-Israeli conflict." This definition also "covers the decedents through the male line of persons who became refugees in 1948." But this is only part of the story. To further explain the complexity on the ground, it is essential to note the following points.

Before we proceed any further, it is imperative to recognize the obvious fact: wars produce refugees. Fear and forced removal of populations are the underlying forces at work. Due to subsequent wars in the region, some of the Palestinian refugees of 1948 experienced refugeehood more than once. That is to say that following the war of 1948 some of those refugees had moved from their original villages and towns located in the current territory of Israel proper, and had resided in refugee camps in the West Bank and Gaza. Following the 1967 war, some of those same refugees moved again into Jordan, East of the Jordan River. Since the West Bank, during the years 1948 to 1988 was under the Jordanian rule, all its residents were granted Jordanian citizenship. Consequently, "refugees" of the 1967 war who moved into Jordan (East of the Jordan River) were referred to as *displaced persons* signifying their status as internally migrant individuals who are distinguished from the refugees of 1948. Again, some, but not all, of those displaced persons were refugees from 1948.

Moreover, following the 1967 war, a group of displaced persons had originated from Gaza. But since Gaza during the years 1948 to 1967 was under the Egyptian rule, those displaced persons were not, and still are not Jordanian citizens but reside in Jordan. This group has the least benefits granted to them by either UNRWA or the Jordanian government.

The result is that Palestinian refugees in Jordan are classified into a number of categories to include refugees, displaced persons from the West Bank, and displaced persons from Gaza. Furthermore, the United Nations has two separate agencies organized to help world refugees. The United Nations Work and Relief Agency (UNRWA) was established in 1949 to carry out direct relief and works programs for Palestine refugees. The second agency is the United Nations High Commissioner for Refugees (UNHCR) was established in 1951 by The 1951 Geneva Refugee Convention following World War II and was charted to protect refugees and assist them with resettlement programs. UNHCR defines a refugee as "A person who is outside his or her country of nationality or habitual residence; has a well-founded fear of persecution because of his or her race, religion, nationality, membership of a particular social group or political opinion; and is unable or unwilling to avail himself or herself of the protection of that country, or to return there, for fear of persecution."[6] Not only that the differences between UNRWA and UNHCR are striking, but also, and most importantly, Palestinian refugees are not covered by UNHCR and are not offered protection or resettlement programs according to its mandate.[7] These distinctions form a hierarchal structure of world refugees in which Palestinian refugees are placed into a second-class refugee status in which Palestinian refugees are not equal in treatment and status to other world refugees. Consequently, their imposed status of refugeehood is designated to a permanent international welfare and relief system that is not mandated to carry out resettlement programs.

Given such reality, the study of Palestinian identity is complicated and is also important and unique in a great number of ways. It is important because the Palestinian problem and the Palestinian-Israeli conflict pose serious political, economic and military challenges to the region and the world. Beyond those global issues, the question of Palestinian identity is unique, differing from that of other groups by the simple fact that Palestinians, through their forced removal, have paid the price for the establishment and the survival of the State of Israel since 1948. Their imposed status is a complex phenomenon that encompasses both their experience with forced migration and their status as refugees. An imposed status removes the option of individual choice from the process of identity formation. Palestinians did not choose to become permanent refugees or displaced persons. They believe that they were forced into this status, and consider the year 1948 the beginning of their *Nakbeh* (Catastrophe). It is important to note that documented history supports Palestinians' claims. The evidence is overwhelming, but for our purposes, it suffices to draw attention to two references: One underscores the findings of *A Survey of Palestine*[8] prepared by the British Mandate for the Anglo-American Committee of Inquiry on Jewish problems in Palestine and Europe, which was later also submitted to the United Nations. According to this survey the Jewish population owned on April 1, 1943 about 5.8% (1,514,247 Dunums[9]) of the total privately owned land of Palestine (26,184,702 Dunums), while the rest of the land (24,670,455 Dunums), about 94%, was the property of Palestinians, and was owned by them. The second reference underlines the work of the Israeli historian, Benny Morris in which he asserts:

"Above all, let me reiterate, the refugee problem was caused by attacks by Jewish forces on Arab villages and towns and by the inhabitants' fear of such attacks, compounded by expulsions, atrocities, and rumors of atrocities, and by the crucial Israeli Cabinet decision in June 1948 to bar a refugee return." (p.38)[10]

Another unique quality of Palestinian identity at this time in history is the fact that not only have most Palestinians become refugees scattered in a number of countries, but that their culture and their identity have also been under siege. Palestinians have experienced personal and collective cultural trauma. Traumas of such magnitude, along with the destruction of their social and cultural institutions, seem to have set the stage for the empty life of refugeehood.

The fact that many Palestinians have become refugees, stateless, and poor makes this research even more unique and of distinct significance. The trauma of *Al-Nakba* is compounded by the number of generations living in refugee camps. Palestinian refugees were not only forced out of their homes and property, but as time passed, had to watch their children and grandchildren born as refugees—many of them also to live in refugee camps. Given that traumatic events have a long-lasting impact on the character and psyche of the individual and on the cultural fabric of society, the question is unavoidable: what is the impact of these events on their identity?

Generally, the largest category of camp-resident refugees represents original Palestinian farming villages. Most of these refugees were land owners and farmers. They lived in small villages scattered throughout historic Palestine. Their families and their villages were the core of their identity, with deep roots that reach far back to ancient Canaanites. Their identities were constructed along their village boundaries. Palestinians made a distinction between the villagers and farmers (*Falaheen*) on one hand, and the city dwellers, or urbanites (*Madanieen*), on the other. Each village had its own traditions, customs, songs, dance, and fables, but all had a connection to Palestine that brought unity among them. Palestinians, like many Arabs of the Middle East, had lived in and experienced a multi-religious society. At the same time, all Palestinians were part of the Arab culture. They spoke Arabic and followed much of Arabic tradition, religion and habit. Cultural norms and taboos were derived from the Arabic culture and reconfigured to meet the expectations of the local village and towns. Jewish-Palestinians, for example, had so much in common with all other Palestinians that they were distinguishable only by their religious practices.

The Palestinian identity therefore was a function of local affiliations mixed with regional and universal features. As a result, Palestinian identity was shaped by four critical circles or spheres: the local community, the larger Palestinian society and culture, and extended Arab/Islamic traditions, and — perhaps most importantly — a special connection to the land. The Palestinian identity was also derived from a deep-rooted relationship with the land. The land of Palestine was not only a source of livelihood, residence and shelter, but also a spring of creation: the land is the root of Palestinian identity. Removing Palestinians from their land might mean the end of their identity.

Ongoing attempts to destroy Palestinian identity that began even before the *Nakbeh* of 1948, were subsequently followed by the never-ending Israeli and Western (The United States included) attacks on Palestinians.[11] For Palestinians, the *Nakbeh* marks a special traumatic point in history because, although Palestine was always a target for invasions and attacks, never before in their modern history were Palestinians forced out of their land or were prevented from returning to it. The *Nakbeh* marks a special point in history that transformed the national, geographic and demographic character of the land. The cumulative results of *Al Nakbeh* and the creation of the refugees' problem led to significant changes including loss of a homeland, destruction of many of those villages, and the formation of an involuntarily-imposed status of refugeehood.[12] In the face of all these changes, the Palestinian identity lives on, and has gotten even stronger and more complex. Benjamin Orbach reports in his collection of letters that, "People here want—no, need—to tell you that they are Palestinians. No matter what state of wealth or poverty they are in, being *Palestinian* is part of their core being."[13]

At the same time, the transformation has been profound, with huge consequences that continue to impact all–Palestinians and non-Palestinians alike throughout the world. It altered the geopolitical, economic, national, and cultural landscape of the region, and transformed international relations.

For Palestinian refugees, the composition of each refugee camp doesn't mirror that of the original villages of Palestine. Camp residents today are four-generation refugees who came from different villages, and are united by their shared experiences of pain, forced removal and refugeehood. They are also united by their dreams and hopes for a better future. Above all they are united by a shared collective memory of their original homeland, Palestine.

At this time in history, where Palestinians consider themselves a nation without a state, their condition in general, and of refugees in particular, can be described as paradoxical and marginal.[14] It is characterized by distinct, conflicting positions within an individual. It is a liminal status of being neither-this-nor-that—neither me nor not-me. Entrapments of such magnitude make Palestinians on the whole and, Palestinian refugees in particular, concurrently visible and invisible. In the end, while their identity may now be in flux, their land remains the core element of their being.

NOTES

1. An extensive account of the history of Palestine can be found at: http://www.salaam.co.uk/themeofthemonth/may02_index.php?l=1 (24 Aug. 2008).

2. The Jewish Virtual Library. http://www.jewishvirtuallibrary.org/jsource/History/palname.html (4 Dec. 2008).

3. John Rose, *The Myths of Zionism* (London: Pluto Press, 2004).

4. United Nations Relief and Work Agency (UNRWA) was established in the wake of the *Nakbeh* of 1948. It is the sole agency to address the humanitarian needs of Palestinian refugees. http://www.un.org/unrwa/publications/index.html (13 Aug. 2008).

5. United Nations Relief and Work Agency (UNRWA), who is a refugees? http://www.un.org/unrwa/refugees/whois.html (15 May 2009).

6. The 1951 Refugee Convention, United Nations High Commissioner for Refugees (UNHCR), http://www.unhcr.org/basics/BASICS/3c0f495f4.pdf (15 May 2009).

7. Convention and Protocol Relating to the Status of Refugees, 1951 Convention, http://www.unhcr.org/protect/PROTECTION/3b66c2aa10.pdf (15 May 2009), p. 5-6.

8. J.V.W. Shaw (ed.), *A Survey of Palestine*: prepared in December 1945 and January 1946 for the Information of the Anglo-American Committee of Inquiry. Reprinted by The Institute for Palestine Studies (Washington, D.C., 1991). Vol. II, P. 566.

The Anglo-American Committee of Inquiry on Jewish Problem in Palestine and Europe was charged to agree on a policy of Jewish immigration to Palestine. Mr. Shaw compiled this survey in his capacity as the Chief Secretary to the Government of Palestine under the British Mandate.

9. Dunum—According to the OnlineUnitConversion website, a "Dunum, also Dunham, is a traditional unit of land area in the Middle East and the Balkans . . . a metric unit equal to 1000 square meters or 0.1 hectare (about 0.2471 acre)." Source: http://www.onlineunitconversion.com/acre.survey_to_dunum.dunham.html (30 September 2008).

10. Benny Morris, "Revisiting the Palestinian Exodus of 1948", pp. 37-59 in *The War for Palestine: Rewriting the History of 1948*, Eugene. L. Rogan and Avi Schlaim (eds.) (NY: Cambridge University Press. 2001).

11. The Balfour Declaration of 1917, written by Arthur James Balfour, Foreign Secretary of England at the time, was given to Lord Rothschild, granting the Jewish people the right to establish a homeland in Palestine.

12. Khalidi documents the destruction of more than 400 Palestinian villages in the wake of 1948. Walid Khalidi, *All that Remains: The Palestinian Villages Occupied and Depopulated by Israel in 1948* (Washington, DC: Institute for Palestine Studies, 1992).

13. Benjamin Orbach, *Live From Jordan: Letters Home from My Journey through the Middle East* (Washington, DC: American Management Association, 2007), 31.

14. Marwan and Tiltnes describe the status of Palestinian refugees in Jordan as marginal. Marwan Khawaja and Åage Tiltnes, eds., *On the Margins: Migration and Living Conditions of Palestinian Camp Refugees in Jordan* Fafo-report 357 (Norway: Centraltrykkeriet, 2002).

Part Two

RESEARCH PLANS
ENCOUNTER REALITY

Chapter Two

Getting In

When news of my research proposal became known at the college where I teach and around town where I live, a number of my colleagues and friends were, of course, very supportive and encouraging, declaring the importance of this topic. Yet attempts to suppress my work were loud and clear: Few persons claimed it was anti-Semitic; some individuals of high position reacted in disbelief, with a passive-aggressive tone of "Ha!?" Others responded somewhat cynically (or perhaps realistically): "Good luck publishing your work!" One individual was verbally hostile and offensive, making a point to provoke me by saying the Israeli Air Force was "the strongest in the region."

As I reflected on my experience, it is imperative to point out that rhetoric of this kind is misleading and misplaced, and is usually raised to divert attention from the real issues and to suppress the underlying reality of the Israeli-Palestinian conflict. Not only are Palestinians also Semites, but Anti-Semitism is rooted in European history. In this context, I recall a passage from Ralph Ellison's *Invisible Man*[1] which describes the hostile, violent reaction to a statement about "social equality" by a young negro:

> The room filled with the uproar of laughter until, no doubt distracted by having to gulp down my blood, I made a mistake and yelled a phrase I had often seen denounced in newspaper editorials, heard debated in private.
>
> "Social . . ."
>
> "What?" they yelled.
>
> ". . . equality"
>
> The laughter hung smokelike in the sudden silence. I opened my eyes, puzzled. Sounds of displeasure filled the room. The M.C. rushed forward. They shouted hostile phrases at me. But I did not understand.

Ellison went on to describe how this young man ultimately had to change his statement from "social equality" to "social responsibility."

Thus, before I had even left my home state of New Jersey, I was reminded that the experience of oppressed groups is similar regardless of their native land. Powerful forces use all means at their disposal—force, education, finances, media, propaganda, and the like—to maintain the *status quo* and preserve their privileges.

I selected Jordan as the site of my research for a number of reasons. First, Jordan has one of the largest concentration of Palestinians outside Israel, the West Bank and Gaza totaling at about 3.5 million. Second, Jordan hosts the majority of Palestinian refugees outside of Palestine/Israel—close to 1.9 million of all Palestinians in Jordan are registered refugees. A total of 335,000 of those refugees reside in refugee camps (UNRWA, 2008)[2]. Third, Jordan is the host of thirteen Palestinian refugee camps.[3]—Some of these camps have existed since the year of the *Nakbeh*, 1948. Fourth, Jordan also has the longest boarder (Map 2.1) with Israel and the Palestinian territories of the West Bank.

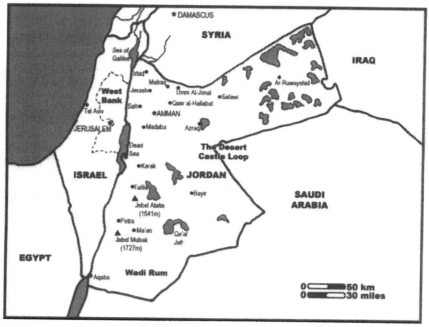

Map 2.1.   Jordan and Surrounding Countries, 2006.

CHALLENGES OF FIELD STUDY

During the months of February through May of 2006, I visited a number of Palestinian refugee camps in Jordan, namely: Irbid Camp; Hitteen Camp, also known as Marka Camp; Jerash Camp, also known as Gaza Camp; and Zarqa Camp. (Map 2.2). I also walked into some of the streets of Al-Hussein Camp and interviewed a refugee from Baqa'a Camp. Throughout my visits to these camps, I observed both the physical space and human interactions, talked to refugees and non-refugees, and discussed their issues with people in positions of authority, *e.g.*, Department of Palestinian Affairs (DPA), UURWA, and university professors.

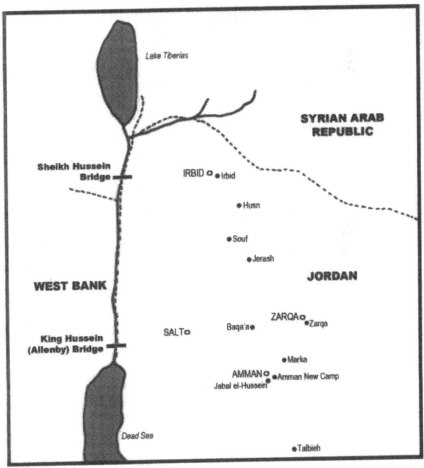

Map 2.2. Location of Ten UNRWA Refugee Camps in Jordan, 2006.

The camps are relatively isolated, conservative, traditional, homogeneous communities. All of the residents are of Palestinian origin and the Muslim faith, but their geographic roots vary. Some are from the Galilee region, the northern part of Palestine; they constitute the majority in Irbid Camp. Others are from the Jaffa and Ramlah region, the central part of Palestine; they constitute the majority in Zarqa Camp. Others are from the southern parts of Palestine, Beir Al Sabea and Gaza; they reside in Jerash Camp. These camp populations represent the old farming communities of the various parts of what was historically Palestine.

My major challenge was to gain access to the camps, to the people who lived there, and to their families. This required establishing trust, and my complex identity—as an American, as a stranger or foreigner, as a male, and as one of Palestinian-Arab heritage who was born in Israel—was an intricate part of the matter. To some it was exotic, while others found it confusing. For some it was a source of suspicion, for others it was an inspiration. I always introduced myself as a Fulbright Scholar from the United States, saying I was there to understand the reality in the camps and its impact on the refugees and their identity. On one occasion, I felt my trust had been established when someone who could relate to my identity reflected my statements in the comment, "You are here to observe and deliver reality as you see it."

THE CONTROL FACTORS

Access to the camps was complicated by a number of factors, one of which I refer to as the "control factor." That is to say, there are a number of institutional and cultural mechanisms of control over the camps and their residents which I had to overcome before I could proceed with my research. Through my inquiries, and in order to follow the proper procedures, I learned that having access to the camps and to the refugees, a permit from the Jordanian Department of Palestinian Affairs (DPA) was required. In support of my project, the director of the Fulbright office in Amman issued an official letter introducing me to the director general of the DPA. I was told to hand deliver the letter. "Don't use the mail service—it may never get there," was the advice I followed.

As I was new in Amman, and as the DPA office was located in the same neighborhood where I was residing, I decided to walk to the DPA office. I was told that the office was located across from the Arab Bank, behind the Chamber of Commerce Building. In Amman, and Jordan in general, people use landmarks, not street addresses, for giving directions. As I approached the area, I could see the building, but I did not know how to get there. Later

I discovered that I should have taken the street at the traffic light up the road. As I walked up and down the street, I could not figure it out. Then, a security guard sitting in a security stand noticed me and offered his help. Gratefully, I told him that I was lost. He was very helpful. "I understand," he said. "Go down the street, get over that low fence and walk across the open field." I tried to do what I was told, but I realized that the "low fence" was actually very high and that the "open field" was fenced in for construction and was also muddy. When I returned to him, he smiled and said: "If you are an old man like me, I'll tell you how to get there under one condition: Don't tell anybody that I told you so." He continued: "Go through the Chamber of Commerce Building. At the reception desk you will find two young women. Don't talk to them. Just keep walking and go through the opposite door in the back." I followed his directions, and it worked.

The male receptionist at the front desk guided me to the third floor. There I found two young women chatting. I introduced myself in Arabic. I was told to always use my title as "Doctor," which is supposed to help. I told the one who paid attention to my presence that I had a letter to deliver to the general director. She extended her hand to receive the letter. She received it and replied, "*Khalas*" (Arabic for "That's all"), and turned her head away from me and proceeded to chat with her friend. "This was rude," I thought to myself. I have never been received with such rudeness. I walked away and took a taxi to my office at the university.

Frustrated, I discussed this incident with a few individuals, who suggested "If you want to receive a different treatment, speak in English." So if I wanted to get through this complex, bureaucratic system, I must use proper titles and speak in English. This is what some may call the "Sir syndrome," which is a product of colonial influences—the mind has been colonized. The master may not be physically present but the mind is still enslaved.

I waited for about a week to call the DPA and ask for an appointment with the director. When I called, I spoke in English. The lady who answered the phone gave me an appointment with the director general for the next day. In our conversation, I asked for her name and responded to her in Arabic. She said, "You have good Arabic for an American." I laughed and thanked her for the appointment.

All those experiences, starting with finding the office location to the "proper" protocol and language, raise serious questions about access to services and the bureaucratic hurdles that could be encountered. Nevertheless, the meeting with the director was pleasant. He offered information and suggested that I call him at any time for further assistance. In our discussion I learned that he is from the Galilee, and is related to one of my former students from the Hebrew University. From that moment on, our relationship became closer. This made my visits to the camps much easier. Bureaucratic control can be eased through interpersonal communications. When the formal becomes informal, the outcome is easily achieved.

The other agency that has a direct interest in the camps is the United Nations Relief and Work Agency (UNRWA). If I were to visit their facilities, I had to obtain their permission which depended on my clearance by the DPA. A month later, I met with the director of public information at UNRWA. The meeting was pleasant, informative and helpful, and he granted me permission to visit the UNRWA installations. He also provided me with a folder that included much needed data about UNRWA and its services.

Palestinian refugees are under the humanitarian care of UNRWA, while other world refugees are cared for by the United Nations High Commissioner for Refugees (UNHCR). UNRWA was established in the wake of the Palestinian *Nakba* of 1948; while UNHCR was established initially to assist European refugees resettle after World War II. UNRWA is an agency—perhaps the only one—that maintains records and data on all Palestinian refugees throughout the Middle East, and is responsible for their humanitarian needs, including food, health, housing, and education. As such, it is believed that UNRWA stands as an essential reminder of the Palestinian *Nakba*, the refugees and the right of return.

In addition to the DPA permit, I had also obtained a supporting document from the Center for Strategic Studies at Jordan University. These documents were supposed to facilitate my interactions in and outside the camps. They also granted me legitimate presence in the camps, and provided me with permit to speak to refugees. As my research proceeded, I sensed there was much anxiety and control over who gets into the camps and for what purpose. Official authorities, so it seems, can determine what a refugee in the camp can and cannot do.

Here was an indication that state and other bureaucratic institutions have taken control of the lives of Palestinian refugees and their interactions. People in the camps are not free. They can have personal guests but they can't decide on their own with regard to matters of research and policy concerning them. Their identity is closely associated with the institutions that govern their affairs. These "control factors" reflect Goffman's[4] concept of total institutions. This concept presents one sociological perspective from which social life can be studied, especially the kind of social life that is organized within the physical confines of a building, plant or an area. Institutions, Goffman argues, have encompassing tendencies and are characterized by the total, almost dictatorial, control exercised over their members.

Moreover, some of the parents and teachers that spoke with me reported that following the peace treaty between Jordan and Israel in 1994, Jordan modified its history textbooks and eliminated those sections or books that addressed the history of Palestine. To gain a better understanding of these matters, I contacted the Ministry of Education to set up an interview. Those who agreed to speak with me were willing to do so only on the condition that I submit a questionnaire for their approval before they could set an appointment with me. I explained to them that my research was not based on a structured survey questionnaire and that an appointment for unstructured interview would really be helpful. Unfortunately, I could not meet their bureaucratic procedures and this prevented me from having that added insight.

A second form of control emanated from cultural patterns. One cultural pattern relates to gender. I had open access to men in the camps. The few who invited me to their homes sat alone with me, without their spouses, mothers, daughters or sisters. The moment I entered the home, women disappeared. This cultural matter posed challenges for my research. Men at times mentioned their spouses without much attention to their existence or contribution. It is in this context that oppression is indeed multidimensional. It emanates from political, cultural, economic and religious forces.

Later, however, arrangements were made for me to meet two groups of women. I wanted to learn about the female perspective. Was it any different from the male's point of view? And what was their role in the process of becoming refugees?

The women I saw in public wore coverings from head to toe. This custom, I learned, is not always for religious reasons. Religious reasons notwithstanding, I was told that because the camps are crowded places with narrow streets and high unemployment, where young men are constantly roaming the streets, women cover themselves for their personal safety and protection. Total conformity to the traditional dress code in the camps may also be a reaction to poverty: a uniform dress code hides inequality. Social pressure is another factor that may explain this conduct. One young woman dressed modestly but in modern fashion and did not cover her hair while indoors; she would cover her hair once she ventured out of the office into the camp. "It is better this way," she said.

Another dimension of control had to do with topics of conversation. In Jordan, one cannot be critical of God or the King. Among the people I interviewed, almost everyone said in so many different ways, "We don't talk politics." Nevertheless, they actually talked about their political experiences and in some cases criticized governments other than their own. After all, the term "refugee" is in and of itself a political concept. It seems that what they had in mind was along the lines of: "With the exception of being critical of Jordan, you can talk about almost everything else."

Well, almost everything. Religion is also a taboo subject—insofar as one does not openly question another's beliefs—although it is present in their daily lives. At times it appears fatalistic, with everything, including salvation, coming from God. In *The Myth of the State*, Ernest Cassirer points out:

> In desperate situations man will always have recourse to desperate means . . . if reason has failed us, there remains always the ultima ratio, the power of the miraculous and mysterious.[5]

These constraints on topics of conversation reminded me of my students back in New Jersey, many of whom came from poor urban neighborhoods. They often argued, "We are not supposed to discuss politics or religion", while those who came from more affluent families with higher educational background challenged this idea by openly pursuing such topics.

THE CAMPS

In addition to my official DPA permit to enter the camps, contacts with public institutions, such as social service agencies and Yarmouk University, facilitated my access to the refugees. My entry into Zarqa, Jerash, and Hitteen refugee camps was made possible through contacts with social support service workers. My access to Irbid Camp was made possible through my affiliation with the Center for the Study of Refugees and Displaced Persons at Yarmouk University in Irbid. A research staffer at the Center accompanied me to the camp to meet the Mukhtar[6] who also serves as the head of the Camp Improvement Committee.

A brief description of each of these four camps is presented below as described in a Department of Palestinian Affairs publication.[7] It is important to note that refugees do not own the land on which their shelters are built. The government of Jordan is responsible for matters of infrastructure—land, water, roads, and so on, while UNRWA is responsible for social, health, and educational services.

Irbid Camp

Irbid Camp was established in 1950, on an area estimated to be 234.322 dunums (57.9 acres), and located 95 kilometers north of Amman. It is adjacent to the city of Irbid, located about 20 kilometers from the Syrian border and about 18 kilometers from the border with Israel. In 2002, the camp population was estimated to be about 23,778, consisting of 4,733 families. Most of the camp dwellers originated from the Palestinian towns and villages of Gaza, Haifa, Faloujeh, Beir Sheba, and Nazareth, having been evicted after the 1948 war. The camp has 1,693 housing units. The area of an average housing unit is 64 square meters.

Hitteen (Marka) Camp

Hitteen Camp was established in 1968, following the 1967 War in an area estimated at 894.632 Dunums (221.07 acres). The camp is located 11 kilometers north-east of Amman and about 15 kilometers south-west of the city of Zarqa. In 2002, it had a total population of about 41,965 people, who originally came from the Palestinian towns and villages of Beir Sheba, Jaffa, Ajour, Dawaymeh, and Deir Nakhass. The camp has a total of 2,824 housing units. The area of an average housing unit is 100 square meters.

Jerash (Gaza) Camp

Jerash (Gaza) camp was established in 1968 on an area estimated at 531.4 dunums (131.3 acres), located 35 kilometers north of Amman, in the valley between the mountains of the city of Jerash (about 7 kilometers from the city). In 2002, the camp population was estimated to be about 14,904, consisting of 2,808 families. Most of the camp dwellers originated from the Palestinian towns of Gaza and Beir Sheba. The camp has 2,130 housing units. The area of the average housing unit is 100 square meters.

Zarqa Camp

Zarqa camp was established in 1949 on an area estimated at 182.589 dunums (45.12 acres), located 25 kilometers north-east of Amman, and about 2 kilometers south-west of the Zarqa city center. In 2002, the camp population was estimated to be about 18,000, consisting of 3,335 families. Most camp dwellers originated from the Palestinian villages of Salama, Beisan, Jaffa, Ramleh, and Lud. The camp has 1,135 housing units. The area of the average housing unit is 100 square meters.

RESEARCH IN THE FIELD

As an exploratory project, the aim of this study is to present a foundation and set a tone for future research. There is much to examine, to explore, and to study, and the door must remain open for future research about many of the questions, hypotheses, and theoretical models as proposed by this project. There are also several methodological issues that are of particular importance to the study of refugees. Their role in this study and their implications for data collection are discussed below.

POLITICAL SENSITIVITIES

First, studying refugees is a very sensitive matter. Refugees are a product of political conflicts. In fact, they are the embodiment of the conflict. Consequently, many parties may have an interest in a particular refugee community. Researchers must always pay attention to those matters and to the conflicting demands. Above all, they must be sensitive to the refugees' feelings of suspicion and mistrust. Researchers might be mistaken for spies. Hence their candid presentation of themselves and their goals is of paramount importance. Moreover, refugees are always at risk. To protect the identity of the refugees I spoke with, I have changed all of their names throughout the text. The pictures presented in this text were taken by me, and represent a sampling of what those housing units look like.

PHYSICAL SPACE AND THE ENVIRONMENT

Initially, I had intended to visit people in their homes. I had planned to sit down with the whole family and record their experiences, ideas and aspirations. But the moment I became aware of the field, I began to realize that this goal might be impossible to achieve. Refugees don't have a home. They rarely stay in their dwellings. They spend most of their waking hours outside their "housing unit," which serve as poor, human "storage units". Refugees roam the streets; children's hopeless, empty eyes; uncollected garbage, crowded streets, and open sewage tunnels are only a few of those features of the camps' environment.

The refugees don't have the space to sit down together as a family. In most cases, children sleep with their parents in the same room. Moreover, the residents experience intrusion on a daily basis—from their neighbors, from strangers, from reporters, and at times from researchers like me. They lack a private time and a private space. Noise is ceaseless.

DATA COLLECTION

The information I gathered was obtained in public. People were eager to speak. In fact, people began to talk to me the moment I said "Hello." They were not hesitant to tell their stories and they were not reluctant to debate their views with others. All was done in public—either in an office or on the street. One exception was the family from Irbid that had moved out of the camp. They had a sense of pride and accomplishment from having worked hard to buy a piece of land and to build their new home.

With the exception of introductory questions, I did not have a predetermined set of questions. I sat down with people and gave them space to talk about their experiences as refugees. In an attempt to understand the personal and the collective narrative of Palestinian refugees, I set out to explore qualitatively their experiences and struggles. I kept my questions open-ended and centered my inquiry on a number of themes including:

History—Why were they forced out of their homeland? How did it happen?
Becoming refugees—What was the journey into refugeehood like? How did they end up in refugee camps?
Life in the camp—What does it mean to be a refugee, stateless and poor? What type of challenges do they encounter daily? Why don't they get out of the camp?
The future—What are their dreams, hopes and aspirations? What options do they see available for them to get out from the oppressive conditions of refugeehood?

There are a number of ways and methods that might shed light on human identity, but in the eyes of this researcher, identity is closely correlated with the individual narrative and the collective memory. For those refugees, telling their story and making it public is in and by itself a journey into their hearts, which will ultimately take the reader into a reality that goes beyond the headlines.

The four months allocated for my research were sufficient enough to begin raising general questions and to explore general themes, but it was not sufficient to conduct full exploration of those themes. By definition, qualitative exploration requires more time. The data you are about to read, at best, scratches the surface, but it provides us with enough information for a better understanding of the Palestinian refugees and their plight.

As I was searching for a simple and direct way to gauge ethnic/national identity, I kept my eyes and ears open to the stories of the refugees. They talked about being Arabs, Muslims, Palestinians, and Jordanians. But, who are they? Do they own up to all these identities? What is their most important identity—the one that guides behavior? And what makes one identity more important than another?

Toward the end of my research journey, which was filled with intense and difficult interviews, I came up with the idea to use an identity circle (Figure 2.1) as a research instrument. This discovery was like one of those unintended

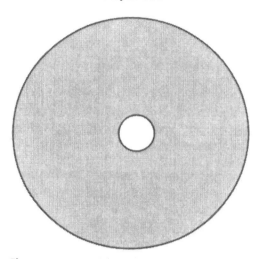

Figure 2.1. Measuring Identity: The Identity Circle. Subjects with multidimensional identity could slice the circle according to their sense of personal affiliation. Palestinian refugees in Jordan, for example, could use this instrument to choose any combination of the following community spheres: Palestinian, Arab, Muslim, and Jordanian.

consequences that have the potential to shape future research on identity. This instrument is in essence an index of individual identity that measures their identification and affinity with their community spheres. I used the identity circle only once and found that (1) it might offer a semi-quantitative measure of identity; and (2), it offers persons with multiple identities an opportunity to slice it according to their definition and perception of themselves. Self-identification is an essential step for an individual to place him/her self in a meaningful place in this large, overwhelming, impersonal, and at times cruel universe. Identity carries within its boundaries history, struggles, pain, victories, defeat, memories and much more. Providing refugees in general—and Palestinian refugees in particular—an opportunity to do so might be a liberating experience, particularly in light of the fact that their identity is constantly threatened with annihilation.

As to research methodology, using the identity circle instrument could easily provide large amounts of data that accurately represent, or at least approximate, reality. Moreover, it could open the door for in-depth discussions with the subjects about their narrative and where they find meaning for their existential struggle. Although this instrument is still in its early stages of development and requires validation, it was valuable to use in that one occasion. I drew a circle and asked that refugee to divide the circle into slices, like pieces of a pie, each representing a dimension of his identities, and estimate the size of each slice: an Arab (ethnic identity); a Muslim (religious identity); a Palestinian (original national identity); and a Jordanian (national identity). He was invited to give each dimension its share—the way he perceived himself, down deep in his heart.

For the most part, the people I interviewed were cooperative and willing to talk without much reluctance. But almost all had the same questions for me in return: "Do Americans really understand our misery? Do they understand the injustices done to us? Do they really care? Can you talk about our reality without any fear or reservations?" I don't think they expected an answer. In their rhetorical nature, those questions implied a deep sense of frustration and disillusionment.

LANGUAGE AND COMMUNICATIONS

Another methodological issue with regard to conducting qualitative research interviews pertains to the language of the community of interest. Language is not limited to its grammatical structure alone, but includes deeper cultural and emotional meanings. It is the understanding of the emotional tone and context that makes all the difference. When refugees spoke about food, children, music or land, for example, their words go beyond their ordinary meaning—they took on a universe of their own with a varied, colorful existence. My fluency in Arabic, English and Hebrew made that understanding possible without the need for a translator.

CULTURAL SENSITIVITIES AND GENDER RELATIONS

One must also be aware of the cultural sensitivities of the community. In the case of Palestinian refugees, matters of gender and religion were very sensitive issues. They were taboo subjects that were not to be raised. As someone of Palestinian heritage who understands the language, culture, and religion, and the *Nakba*, I was also an American, a male, and a foreigner. With the exception of meeting women in formal office settings, with men present, I did not meet women in their homes. Special arrangements were made for that purpose.

A woman who works in the social services field invited four women to meet with me in her office, but accommodations were made to meet in a refugee's residence because of an elderly woman who could not walk up to the office. A second meeting with another group of five women was held in an office. In both cases, a young male resident, Hussein, who served as my companion at Hitteen Camp, was present at those meetings. His presence did not seem to make a difference in the women's narratives, but it seems that he was there to guard the cultural standards of gender interactions.

BUREAUCRATIC AND FORMAL SYSTEMS

Researchers must be aware of the bureaucratic and formal systems that deal with the community of interest. This area has its own rules, language, guidelines and policies that may impact their research. Jordan has its own political history, social structure, institutions, and organizations. To carry out my research plans effectively, I had to be aware of the formal and informal social and political systems, of the tribal structure of the society, of the history of Jordan with the Palestinians and of the conflicts that exist in that society. I had also learned about their emphasis on informal and process interactions over the formal guidelines. Studying a specific community in any given society should not be done in a vacuum. That community must be placed in its proper context.

SELF AWARENESS

Finally, the role of researcher in the research process itself requires acute self-awareness. Objectivity in such a milieu, I argue, is greatly dependent on self awareness of one's values and research objectives. For example, the more often I visited the camps the less shocked I became. My initial anxiety subsided. I did not know if that was good or bad, but I was disappointed. How could I accept this miserable reality? As a person who believes in human dignity, how could I accept misery as a given. This worried and confused me. Did I truly accept it?

The gravity of reality is such that people have a tendency to adapt to even the most oppressive conditions. Thus, I mused: Although I must find a way to feel comfortable with my research and interactions with the refugees, I must not accept the misery of the camps. After all, this is not about me. As a researcher, my responsibility is to deliver a picture of that reality the way I find it, just as a photographer produces excellent pictures of his objects without him being present in those pictures. I am also the one to provide a context and interpretation for that reality according to scientific principles, within the proper historical context, and consistent with the theoretical frameworks with which I am familiar. By doing so, I also gave myself the hope that my work could provide an impetus for change.

NOTES

1. Ralph Ellison, *Invisible Man* (New York: Vintage Books, 1947, 1980), 31.

2. United Nations Relief and Work Agency (UNRWA). http://www.un.org/unrwa/publications/index.html (13 Aug. 2008).

3. Only ten out those thirteen camps are recognized by UNRWA. The other three camps were established and are administered by Jordan. UNRWA may provide some welfare services to the residents of those camps.

4. Erving Goffman, "On the Characteristics of Total Institutions," in *Asylums: Essays on the Social Situation of Mental Patients and Other Inmates* (New York: Anchor Books, A Division of Random House, 1961), 1-124.

5. Ernest Cassirer, *The Myth of the State* (New Haven: Yale University Press, 1966), 279.

6. *Mukhtar*, literally means "the chosen one." It is an official title given to the head of the largest or strongest family in the village. The term is derived from the Ottoman Empire era when heads of villages were appointed by the Turkish ruler to represent their respective villages.

7. Hashemite Kingdom of Jordan, Department of Palestinian Affairs, *55 Years in Serving Refugee Camps*, 2003.

Part Three

VOICES FROM THE CAMPS

Chapter Three

Zarqa Camp, February–March 2006

The taxi rolled into the camp. I did not know what to expect. I had never seen so many people in such a small area. The street was suddenly narrow and packed with people young and old—men, women and children. The place looked dark with little stands of a variety of products for sale. Almost all of the women were dressed in dark long robes. With the exception of their faces, they were *muhajabat* (Arabic from Hijab, veil). I was concerned of accidents with children running around on the street or with cars driving in the opposite direction on a very narrow road. It is a new reality, a new way of life—it is a refugee camp. I began to return to my senses, and questions ran through my mind. What does it feel like to live in such a crowded environment? How have the people managed to survive for more than sixty years in such conditions?

We didn't have to drive far or deep into the camp. The driver turned left from the highway, crossed over railroad tracks, turned left again, and immediately right. As the driver didn't know the exact location of the UNRWA offices and the Women's Center, I called them for directions.

They started with their introductions the moment that I arrived. They were quick. The office furniture included a desk, a computer, a telephone, a gas-operated mobile heating unit and chairs. The facility is of simple construction with thin walls that look as if they are going to fall down any moment. It lacks men's facilities and running water. It reminded me of some of the shacks one can find in rural Appalachia and of some Native American reservations in the United States.

My hosts were curious and eager to learn about my objectives and the time I planned to spend in the camps. There was a sense of openness and trust in the air. I spoke their language and was quick to use the cultural nuances—the looks, the handshake, the gestures and the command of common phrases.

Photo 3.1. Kitchen in Zarqa Camp, 2006.

There were five people in the room. There was Issa who is a practicing local attorney. He had moved out of the camp to Alzarqa, an adjacent city to which the camp was named after. Samiha was also there; she is a mother of two beautiful boys who went in and out of the room during our meeting. They were very polite, shaking hands with me when she introduced us. Samiha was born in a village near Bethlehem after the Israeli occupation of the West Bank and Gaza in 1967. After getting married she moved into Zarqa camp. She now resides outside the camp with her family.

The third was Ibtisam, a young mother of a four-year-old daughter named, A'kka, who is named after the ancient coastal Palestinian city, Acre (A'kka is Arabic for Acre). Ibtisam said that she heard people were told to stop naming their children after Palestinian landmarks or towns. Finally, there were Jameela and Fatima, single women who work in the field of women's empowerment and childcare.

VOICES OF IDENTITY

The discussion was intense. Issa was smoking, and they argued back and forth about a number of issues, including the right of return. Should people have to stay locked in refugee camps to claim their right? Or should they get out, advance their personal lives and maintain their attachment to their homeland? The views varied, but Jameela asserted, "One doesn't have to live in oppressed conditions to express one's nationalism," adding, "Edward Said[1] was a man who lived in complete comfort and freedom, yet loved his nation and helped the Palestinian cause." They said that camp residents are divided over this issue.

They spoke of loss and deprivation and were passionate about their predicament. They feel not only that the world ignores the plight of Palestinian people, but Palestinians are now divided into so many groups that it is difficult to feel as one nation or one people. Some Palestinians live in Gaza, completely isolated from other Palestinians; others live in refugee camps in Lebanon and Syria, the West Bank, and Jordan. They observed that different groups of Palestinians live in different countries under different rules, all of which add to the complexity of the situation. Samiha added: "Families are divided. What do you expect? They all feel that they ought to resist these conditions, but their circumstances make it difficult to organize and to follow one path."

A feeling of sadness and confusion was in the air. Someone commented that, "It seems that all that is left of Palestine is the symbol, the idea. Now that we cannot name our children after Palestinian landmarks and towns those symbols will also be taken away." Issa added that there is a movement of *Tawteen* (settlement of Palestinians in their host countries) which may cause even more tension and add to the trauma. People, for example, may have to choose between being Palestinian or Jordanian. "This is not an easy thing for us. Why can't we have both?" he questioned.

With regard to relations with the Jordanian people and government, my hosts felt that young Palestinians identify themselves more as Jordanians than as Palestinians. Children listen to the stories of their elders and think they are just "fables, myths." They are now about sixty years removed from the original tragedy.

With regard to employment and the economy, the poverty is obvious. People work in private trade jobs and little stands in the camp. They feel that they don't have equal access to government or public jobs. "Discrimination is obvious," my hosts asserted.

With regard to religion, my hosts argued that religiosity is on the rise for a number of reasons. First, all other social institutions that hold society together have failed them, but religion is still a secure and stable institution. Second, the ongoing pressure by Israel and the West on the Arab and Islamic world in general has led to a stronger Muslim identity. Third, people need hope. In desperate situations religion provides hope.

Listening to these emotional discussions, I asked, "How does a Palestinian man or woman in the camp sort all these matters out? How do they deal with it? How do they explain it?" Their answer was simple: "They ignore it! Don't think about it." But people care very much about their identity card issued by UNRWA to each registered refugee. Issa said that his grandmother considers it "sacred."

I asked to see one. Samiha showed me hers. It is a simple piece of paper that looks official with entries of names, address, children, and the like. The headings are written in both English and Arabic, but the entries giving specific individual information are written only in English. "Perhaps some people can't read English!" I said. They looked puzzled and said nothing. However, they added that there are refugees who are not registered with UNRWA, notably those who are refugees of the 1967 war. Issa commented that a distinction is made between a refugee (*Lage'a*) and a displaced person (*Nazeh*): "A refugee is one who was forced out in 1948, while a *Nazeh* is one who left the West Bank after 1967 war and went to other parts of Jordan. It is a form of internal displacement."[2]

As we sat there, Um Ibrahim, an older woman, dressed in black, walked in twice to serve coffee and tea. Later, about 2:30 in the afternoon they brought individual packages of what I would describe as "McDonald's look-alike food," made by a local establishment called Balady, and small cans of Pepsi, Sprite, and the like. They had fried chicken with fried potatoes. We shared the meal together.

As I walked out, there were two children playing with an empty soda can on the bare front concrete floor. Issa and Fatima accompanied me to the taxi that was waiting for me right by the door. I requested to take pictures of the street outside. They gave me a gesture as if to say, "Why not, why ask?"

VOICES OF OPPRESSION

At a later visit, I had a further discussion with Samiha, who spoke about conditions in the camps and some of the problems of the camps' population: First, the poverty rate is high and the poor live in misery. Poverty, she claims, brings additional problems. When a man finds himself powerless, he runs away from home, leaving his wife and children behind. It also brings family tension and domestic violence. Drug use is also high.

Second, the quality of life for children is poor. Students' dropout rate is high. Schools are so crowded that UNRWA offers a two-shift school day (8:00 am to Noon, and Noon to 4:30 pm). Thus, many children spend most of their time out in the streets. Child labor is also high, as is early marriage for daughters. I mentioned that in Amman I had seen a television advertisement promoting control of this phenomenon, so it seems that it is not limited to camp residents. Samiha agreed and explained that early marriage is a common phenomenon in Jordan and that, "There are Jordanian villages that are actually worse than the refugee camps."

In the middle of the conversation, others walked in and the discussion became more casual and more general. A heavy-set man with a cigarette in his mouth was introduced to me as Zein. He was a non-stop smoker. Issa, the lawyer, also arrived with a cigarette in his mouth. Consequently, two of the six who were in attendance were smoking in the office. (One cannot ask people to stop smoking – it is common throughout the Kingdom. People smoke everywhere except on public transportation, where it is illegal). Samiha told me that Zein had agreed to be my companion for the day and he would take me to visit his family as well.

Samiha, Zein and I walked out together to the Department of Palestinian Affairs (DPA) office. We walked through little narrow alleys and narrow streets. They told me that the camps are built in rows of housing blocks. Zarqa Camp has thirteen rows. It has a population of about 18,000, living in housing units that range in size from 50 to 90 square meters. All of the streets were narrow with the exception of one. They explained that that particular street had some other structures in the past which were recently removed leaving the street wider than the rest.

I don't really know how to describe the scene. I believe that words do not adequately describe such conditions. The whole area is dry. Not a living tree is standing. Plants and animals are not to be seen. There is no life except walking human bodies. Zein said, "There is no room to plant anything." Everything looks gray—dirty and dusty. Unemployment is high. Children, men and women hang out on street corners since the "houses" are too small to stay inside.

Zein lives with his family of ten in a 70-square-meter unit (753 square feet). He is a fifty-year-old married man who lives with his wife, their seven children, and his mother. His family became refugees from Ramleh in 1948, after Israeli troops invaded the area. They have been in this camp ever since. They lost their forty dunum (9.9 acre) land in Palestine, their house and everything they owned. His father is deceased and they do not have the resources to get out of the camp. He asserted, "The camps are here to stay until a resolution to the Palestinian-Israeli conflict is reached. But people are free to get out if they can afford to do so." There are some people who have managed to save and get out, but they are few. The majority are left behind, trapped in the camps.

We walked to the DPA camp office. It looked spacious and many residents were walking in to take care of their official business. We met a number of men sitting in the office. The Committee responsible for managing the camp has twelve members appointed by the DPA central office. I was told that one woman currently serves on the Committee. When I questioned this fact, the answers were varied. "The maximum we had on the Committee at any given time was three women," said one. "It is a matter of tradition that women are less likely to serve in public office," said another. "It is a matter of ability, not tradition, to serve on this Committee; one has to have leadership qualities," said a man who had been quiet throughout the meeting.

"Does that mean that women lack such qualities?" I asked.

The answer was silence.

Changing the subject to the conditions in the camp, there was much talk about the need for improvement but also much praise given to the Committee. They actually praised themselves and recited a number of improvements that had been made such as street paving, sewerage, running water, and power.

Turning to the refugees, in the Director's words, "Refugees are the least fortunate." People live in small, crowded housing units—a situation that causes tension, family problems, and quarrels between neighbors. "If you cough in your home, your neighbors can hear you," he explained. The walls are very thin and simply made of wood. There is no privacy. In the winter, roofs leak. Many poor families, particularly older widows, cannot afford the cost of roof repairs, so they live under the sky.

The income of camp residents is very low. Many make less than JD100 (USD140) a month, but some make close to JD150 (USD211) a month. Only a few have succeeded to acquire better positions and save some money. "Those people have moved out to the city," he explained.

There are no parks or central entertainment places for families or children. Most people spend their time out on the street. The streets are very narrow. Ambulances and fire engines, when needed in an emergency, cannot pass through. Because of such conditions, people are over-stressed. Many get sick and the health services are poor. Also, if one gets sick, the whole camp might get sick as well—contagious conditions spread fast.

As to their experience of being refugees in Jordan, members of the committee reiterated similar themes as Issa, Samiha, Ibtisam, Jameela and Fatima had touched upon:

Most of us in this camp came from Jaffa, Lud and Ramleh region of Palestine. We were forced out in 1948.

Our families left their property under fear and persecution. They were told that it was a matter of days until they would return home. Today we feel that nobody cares about our cause.

Religion is on the rise. People have lost hope—their only hope (now) is in God.

With regard to matters of identity, the head of the committee, who is of Jordanian ancestry and never lived in the camp, plainly asserted, "Refugees have dual identity." The rest in the room, all of Palestinian origin remained quiet. They did not challenge or support this notion.

The schools' curricula had included courses on the history of Palestine, but after the Peace Agreement between Jordan and Israel,[3] those courses were removed. "Our children don't know the story," they said, "so it is left up to the individual family to teach their children about their roots and about the *Nakba*."

During the discussion, I noticed Zein was getting a bit edgy. I signaled to him that we should be leaving shortly. At that moment, some were curious about my identity and purpose. Although I had introduced myself and gave everyone in attendance my Fulbright business card, I explained the matter again. The director had excused himself from the meeting, apologizing that he had to attend another meeting that was scheduled a day earlier. He added, "The rest will spend some time with you and answer your questions."

Suddenly, a young man walked straight up to my face questioning my purpose there. I stood up and, for the third time, explained to him and to the rest of the group my purpose and my affiliation. I was a bit nervous and told them that my visit was approved by the DPA central office. Some people laughed with embarrassment and explained that this young man is just "doing his job." Zein was annoyed with what had happened and almost screamed at this young man, "Do your job with proper manners!" which brought an end to our meeting.

Zein was not happy with my visit to the DPA office from the start. He tried to prevent me from going there. "They are all crooks. They embezzle charity contributions and take them to their families and friends," he said. Zein also pointed out that the episode with that young man was a setup. "The man who had spoken about women not having leadership qualities had moved over to the director's chair after the director left and had secretly requested this young man to come in and question you."

"How did you know?" I asked curiously.

"You were busy talking and taking notes. I saw the signaling," Zein said.

He turned out to be correct. The next morning I received a phone call from the director. He apologized again for leaving early and for the "incident," as he called it, and continued, "It is really not the young man's fault. It is the fault of some members who think in awkward ways." Again he conveyed his apology and extended an invitation for me to visit at any time.

Two days later, I received a phone call from the DPA Director General. He wanted to "check on me," he said. We talked about my work and my visits to the camps. I thought that for my own protection I should inform him of the "incident." I did not know if he knew about it or not, but he said, "Things might happen. Let me know if you encounter any problems."

Although this incident raised some concerns about my personal safety, it also made me wonder about how oppressed people end up policing each other. The mere fact that committee members are appointed by the national office speaks volumes as to the potential use of power against the population.

A VOICE OF HOPELESSNESS

It was past noon and I told Zein that I would be honored to visit his family today and that I might have to come back to meet with other families. He said, "I want you to meet this man, then we'll come back to my home." We walked in the street to get to the house. Zein knocked at a small metal door and called out: "Jamal!" An older-looking, skinny, unshaven man with a cigarette in his mouth opened the door and welcomed us to enter.

The door was narrow and so low that in order for me to get in I had to turn to the side and lower my head. We walked into a small open space—big enough for two people. To the right was his bathroom. Next to that was his kitchen and across from it was his bedroom. The total living space in this unit measured 50 square meters (538 square feet). To enter his bedroom (living room), we took off our shoes. Inside was a single-size bed, a mattress on the floor, and a small closet. That is all. There was no more space. Zein and Jamal sat on the mattress on the floor and invited me to sit on the bed. A number of pictures were hung on the walls. There was no window. There was no shower. The ceiling looked as if it was going to fall down. There was hardly any room to move around. The bed extended from one end of the wall to the other—it took up half the space. Both men were smoking like chimneys and there was a little kerosene-operated heating unit.

Jamal was born in 1946 in Ramleh, Palestine, but looks much older than his chronological age. His parents fled their home because of fear of persecution. "We owned about 12 dunums (2.97acre) of grapes and orchards, but they left everything behind," he said. "Our parents told us that people were saying that the Jewish soldiers were raping our women and killing our men. Violation of family honor (*A'rd*) is a taboo." About his guilt over his anger with his parents, he said, "Family honor is the only excuse I give my parents for leaving their homeland." The family fled on a donkey to Gaza, where they lived for about two years before leaving again for Zarqa Camp. "We have been here ever since," he said. "My parents are dead. I married once, and my wife died two months later. I remained single."

Jamal is a bitter man but maintains his sense of humor. He lives on little money and rations from UNRWA. He is frustrated and seems to have lost all hope. "What hope?" he questioned and added, "Nobody cares about our cause. We all will die here in our misery." He was instrumental in the Fatah movement and talked about his past commitment for change. "Many leaders came and slept in this bed – right here," he said with mixed feelings. He showed me letters (which I did not read) from Palestinian "leaders" recognizing his work, but he rejected all they had to offer him. He has lost sympathy for them because, in his words, "They were not honest."

A VOICE OF SHAME

We departed Jamal's "home" and went to visit Zein's home. The front metal door is covered with a big textile sheet to protect the house from dust. There I met one of his sons and his youngest daughter. He seemed to be a very loving father. He told me that his son was injured at home and he didn't have enough money to provide for his treatment. He explained, "Refugees don't have medical insurance," and the cost of surgery and medication exceeded JD 10,000. He looked embarrassed but added, "I appealed to the Royal Court, but nothing came out of it. Finally, a friend of mine sponsored his medical expenses. My friend came back from the United States where he had made some money. I was ashamed but I had no choice. My friend told me, 'Your son is our son.'"

His children requested that I take pictures of their birds, which I did. I was happy to see an animal. "There is life, albeit in a cage," I thought to myself. The children were very happy to have them and wanted me to take more pictures with them, as if to make them live forever. I didn't meet the rest of Zein's family. I didn't meet his wife or his mother. I noticed, however, that when he took me to see the other room in his small housing unit, he spoke with a loud voice and the door between them was suddenly closed.

Zein has the spirit of an entrepreneur. He owns a little stand right outside his home where he sells used clothing. His children help out in this little "store," as well. To get out to the street, Zein invited me to follow him to the back of the house where there was a big window to go through. He told me that at some point they were not allowed to build those steps below the window. They were penalized by UNRWA. "Now it is OK," he confirmed. So we had to almost crawl through this window to get out to the street.

A VOICE OF BUILDING BRIDGES

Mohammad is a young journalist who covers the refugees and the refugee camps in Jordan. I met him at Zarqa Camp at the Women's Center. He was covering a "graduation" party for a group of teenagers who had completed a training program, sponsored and run by the Center, focusing on HIV prevention and the dangers of drug use. Mohammad, who has Jordanian roots, is married to a Palestinian woman. They have three children, two girls and a boy. He believes that "mixed marriages" are essential for cutting down on racism in Jordan; it is a bridge-building act. He explained that, although there is a tendency not to show it, racism is in fact present. "They even use colors to refer to different groups: the color blue refers to Jordanian, while the color green refers to Palestinians."

Mohammad is also aware of the familial connections between Jordanian and Palestinian families, particularly wealthy families. Yet, he claims, "The Arab regimes work to preserve their own interest, thus causing harm to the people. There is a huge gap between the regimes on one hand and the Arab people on the other. But the gap is not as big in Jordan."

"How does Jordan benefit from the Palestinian refugees?" I asked.

"They will benefit from future reparation programs. If and when it is set, compensation will not only be given to individuals but also to the host countries," he replied.

Mohammed described Jordanians as a tribal people. In speaking of the tensions that must be moderated for there to be unity among groups in Jordan, he also advocated that Palestinians in Jordan not be denied a right of return:

Many Jordanians live in poor rural areas. Their socioeconomic conditions are not much different from those living in refugee camps. In Jordan almost everybody suffers. In addition to the external pressures placed on Jordan, there are internal forces that may contribute to tensions between Palestinians and Jordanians. Both external and internal forces stem from political and economic interests.

This is the reason Jordan is trying to build one nation. It now includes people from different parts of the Arab world. His Majesty, King Abdullah II, has come up with (the) "Jordan First" motto. The intention is to bring unity and to minimize tension between the various national groups. Even the Jordanian army is called 'the Arab Army.' It is all-inclusive. But 'Jordan First' doesn't mean that Jordan should become the alternate nation for the Palestinians. Palestinians have their right of return, and that must be protected until it is fulfilled.

A VOICE OF JUSTICE

As the graduation party ended, I found myself standing next to a young man dressed in tight clothes. His hair was cut short and precisely combed. I asked him about his connection to this party. He replied, "I am a counselor to this group." His name was Hussein. He was born in 1979 in Hitteen Camp, which he described as "a can of sardines. People are jammed in it and they hardly have room to breathe."

Hussein had recently graduated from law school in Syria, and was now preparing for his Jordanian bar exam. His father died in 1980, and his mother in 1998. His face tells the story. He is tense and frustrated but keeps hope alive. Like many camp residents I have met, he hardly smiles; and when he does, it is usually a shy smile. He is the youngest of six children—three brothers and three sisters. Two of his brothers are lawyers and one is a businessman. Two of his sisters are school teachers and the third is a housewife. Together, they represent a story of success, achieved through determination and hard work. "I have been working and going to school since I was eight years old," Hussein stated with pride.

According to Hussein, about two-thirds of the camp population is under the age of thirty. He clarified that having large families is a tradition that is difficult to change. "People believe that children are '*Ozwa*' (Arabic and Hebrew for strength—Oz). Children could be a source of labor and income to the family."

Hussein defined himself as an Arab with a Palestinian-Jordanian identity. He believes that because every person has his own religion, religion should not play an important role in human identity: "All people of faith, whether they are Muslims, Jews or Christians have the right to live. The Palestinian problem is not grounded in religion.—It has to do with land and dispossession.

"What does it mean to be a refugee?" I asked.

Hussein replied with a sense of righteousness, "Children of the camp are children of pain and suffering. They live a reality that is not theirs. When people are forced out of their land, home, and property, they end up living a life removed from their own reality. People love their land and everyone here in the camp wants to return home. For myself, I just want the chance to return home. That is my basic right. I need to decide whether to stay in Jordan or return to my home in Faloujah" (his Palestinian village).

He continued, explaining with a keen sense of justice,

> Freedom is not limited in time. Every person here is aware of the history, and everyone will work hard to keep that history alive. When I say that I want the

right to return home, they label me a terrorist. I am not a terrorist. I just want
to return home. My family's home and land were taken away from us by force.
Justice must be restored. I can never forget oppression and the camp life.

Palestinians have the right of return and the right for compensation. All
should be compensated for their pain. But as to the right of return, it is a private
matter. The right of return should be granted to all, but each individual will have
to make his own decision. All we have now is to insist on our rights and to resist
further dispossession.

"What is life like in the camp? How would you describe it?" I asked. Hussein replied:

As a child of the camp, I volunteer my time to serve at the youth club here.
Refugee camps have many problems—overcrowded neighborhoods, poverty,
narrow and dirty streets, child labor, open sewage. There is ignorance, pain
and suffering. Jordan needs to do more to improve the conditions of the camps.
There is a high rate of unemployment, and crowded schools.

I don't think they should demolish the camps, but they should improve them.
Camps are symbols of the Palestinian cause. We should make a distinction between improvement and final settlement in Jordan or any other country. I am for
improvement but not for such settlement.

Most Jordanians live as refugees. Jordan has two distinct classes: The upper
class makes up about five to ten percent of all Jordanians and Palestinians. The
rest, about eighty to eighty-five percent live under the poverty line. The middle
class has disappeared. There are only the very rich and the very poor. Of course,
the refugees have a higher rate of poverty.

The Palestinian Authority (PA) is not doing things right. They just had an
election. They claim they speak for all Palestinians. But how could they say that,
if I and all refugees in Jordan, Lebanon, Syria and elsewhere did not even have
the opportunity to vote? The PA is itself an entity under occupation. Everything
under occupation is null and void. Since my father passed away when I was one
year old, it was my mother who told me the story of Palestine. I will make sure
to pass it on to my children. One cannot lose hope."

A VOICE OF DEPRIVATION

For my last few visits to Zarqa Camp, I had taken a taxi to and from Amman.
For this visit, I decided to take the bus. I want to understand the ways of the
general public. Not only have I come to learn that taxi drivers were not so
pleasant and overcharged me, but taking a taxi to a refugee camp also looks
elitist.

I took a taxi to Abdali, the local bus station in Amman. It is a noisy and
dirty station. Nevertheless, I inquired about the bus to Zarqa. A young man

standing next to the designated bus, a small minibus that accommodates about twenty passengers, was helpful. Later, I understood that he works on this bus as an assistant to the driver. He was in charge of collecting the fare and opening the door for passengers to get on and off the bus. This was a thirty minute bus ride to Zarqa station.

The Zarqa bus station is also noisy and not clean. It is adjacent to the refugee camp and there is a concrete wall of about four meters high separating the two. At an opening through this wall, an older man was sitting behind a little candy stand. I asked him if I was going in the right direction. He said, "This is the entrance to the camp."

I walked into a little alley made of concrete. There were little housing units on the left and a wall on the right. I followed the path. Two women with their children were also walking in the same direction. About two minutes later I arrived at an open street. I saw UNRWA signs. At the end of that street I also saw commercial stands which looked recognizable. I was familiar with the other end of the street. I walked up the road to the Women's Center where I met Samiha and Fatima.

After we had the traditional Arabic coffee, Samiha accompanied me to the office of the UNRWA Camp Director. Samiha is a young mother who lives outside the camp. She dresses in a modern, but modest style. She wears jeans and doesn't cover her hair. But every time she walks outside the office, she puts a scarf over her head. I asked her about this practice, and she answered, "It is better this way." Today was not an exception.

The director's office was a short distance down the road. Ibrahim was very pleasant and welcoming. He offered to spend the day with me, saying. "I am at your service." He is a forty-seven-year-old gentleman. He wears eye glasses and was dressed in a suit, a tie and an overcoat. It was a bit chilly, and the weather for the last few days had been raining and cold. People told me that these conditions were atypical for the season.

Ibrahim's family fled from their original home in Maghlas, near Al-Khalil (Hebron) in 1948. He claims that atrocities were not committed in their village, but most people fled based on fear of war crimes committed against Palestinians in other parts of the country. They were mostly afraid of rape. "People were simple at the time," he said.

They became refugees in Jericho, where they resided in a refugee camp until the war of 1967, when Israeli planes bombarded the area. They fled again, this time to Jordan:

> I remember the time following the 1967 war when we were attacked and walked on foot to cross the Jordan River. I was eight years old at the time. I couldn't walk, but I had to. The bridge was not stable and I was afraid. My father carried some stuff on his back and my mother helped with the children. We were four

boys and three girls. Finally, we arrived at Karameh in Jordan. They sent all refugees to the school. Days later, they moved us out temporarily to the school yard. From there they moved us to Hitteen Camp, where we have resided ever since. My father worked hard and long hours to provide for the family. I recall at times he took the children with him to work.

His father and mother are in their seventies and both in poor health. Three of his siblings have passed away, and two of his brothers and their families live together in the camp with his parents. "It is a very crowded place. Since I joined the Jordanian army, I moved out of the camp, and now I live with my wife on the outskirts of Amman," he stated.

Ibrahim talked about his seven-year service in the Jordanian army and his four years of work in Saudi Arabia. "I really didn't live in the camp for a long time. I distanced myself from it, and now I live with my wife outside the camp. But the camp is part of my belonging and identity," he stated affirmatively. He is married but has no children. They spent most of their savings on fertility treatment to no avail. With pain in his voice, he explained, "We really wanted children. Not having children in this society is a difficult matter, particularly for women. People intrude into your private and personal business. They want to know everything. Women ask my wife, 'Who is to blame?' They make her feel bad."

He describes life in the camp as difficult, tough and poor. People live in misery.

Some people in the camp live in those poor housing conditions in the same unit with chicken and sheep. I don't know how they make it. We here at UNRWA try to help as much as we can, but our resources are limited. We offer medical care and hospitalization assistance for about seventy-five percent of the cost, up to a maximum of JD100 (USD141). This is really nothing. Each hospitalization costs at least JD300 (USD423). So people avoid medical treatment. People are poor and sick. Most people live on less than JD200 per month. Only a few families are doing well. Some of those families try also to take advantage of the system. That makes me upset. Some families take their children out of school so they can use them as a source of income. Children go out to work and at times some families drag their children along to gain sympathy and to beg for money. Many camp children engage in vandalism; they have no sense of belonging and they spend much of their time outside the home. Fathers work long hours. Some of them are alcoholics. Alcoholism destroys the family. It leads to financial, emotional and family troubles. The family breaks down. Girls remain single. Men won't marry a woman whose father is alcoholic. It brings shame on the family.

As I listened, some of the images reminded me of the inner-city neighborhoods back home in the United States or perhaps a Native American reservation, or the suburbs of Paris. This is the tragedy of the urban poor, of refugees, and of displaced people alike. This is a classic example of what sociologists call *anomie*—conditions of instability in society caused by the erosion or abandonment of moral and social codes; it is a feeling of disorientation and alienation from society caused by the absence of a supporting social or moral framework.

On our way to the school nearby, he said: "The old days were much better. There was much more enthusiasm, attachment and commitment. There was more patriotism. Now they teach a 'peace curriculum' which really doesn't offer much except some ideas about human rights, and the rights of the children." He explained that the Palestinian cause seems to have died after 'Black September'[4] leaving behind a shift in group identity and sense of belonging:

> Now there is more emphasis on individualism and survival of the individual, and not much on a community's belonging to a larger cause. Even the accent is different. Our parents speak in full Palestinian accent, while their children speak in Palestinian-Jordanian accent. For example, *Kaseh* is Jordanian for cup, and *Cubayeh* is Palestinian for cup. Children don't know where they actually belong.

He described life for Palestinians in Jordan as transient:

> People want to return to Palestine. But I recall there was a rumor one day that Palestinians will receive reparation and compensation for loss of property and suffering. Most of the refugees came to the office to make sure that their papers were in order. So it is difficult to predict what people might do. But those who have a strong attachment and value their principles will not accept compensation for property and reparation. It would mean giving up on the dream and on Palestine. There is also the problem of discrimination here in Jordan. At times it is blatant and at times it is not so obvious. But it is there. Refugees are thankful for the host country but they are not fully Jordanians.

As to the future of the camps, he concluded: "Despite all that, the camps are the only witness to the crimes committed against the Palestinians. They must remain until the final solution. They are the only witness to my rights."

At the end of the day, Ibrahim drove me to my apartment in Amman. On our way, he pointed out his apartment, located near the outskirts of Amman, which he rents for JD100 per month. He also talked about how his father had worked for families in Shmaisani, an upscale neighborhood in Amman:

> He took care of their gardens. I recall how many times we were out there working hard and were hungry, but my father wanted to stay out there a little longer, do a little more work. He had to provide for the family. But there were also times

when I cried, secretly. I was jealous of the children in those neighborhoods. 'Why do we have to be poor, hungry and deprived?' I used to ask myself. 'Why do we have to be strangers?' I have always wondered.

VOICES OF MEANING

Ibrahim and I walked together half a block up the road to the Boys School for students in the third through the tenth grades. The building is made of concrete and is surrounded by a concrete wall. The school grounds are made of concrete as well. The light blue UN color identifies the facility as does the UNRWA flag. Students have painted a number of flags on the interior wall of the school yard including the Jordanian and the Palestinian flags. A welcoming sign was posted by the main door to the school, reading "Welcome to Our School."

The principal, Hassan, came out of his office to greet us in the corridor of the first floor. He was pleasant and energetic and had much to say. He welcomed us into his office. Staff and teachers walked in and out, and he paid attention to everyone and provided assistance when needed.

From the appearance of the school it was obvious that this school was distinct, and the teachers and the principal alike described it as a "good" school. They offer a one-shift school day, while almost all schools in refugee camps offer a two-shift school day. The classrooms are spacious enough to accommodate forty-five students, while other schools have smaller and poorer facilities in which students are squeezed together in classrooms. There is a low rate of violence, vandalism and crime. Students also engage in tutoring others and in taking part in teaching about AIDS, drugs and other problems; they encourage prevention. Ibrahim said that "this success was due to the energy, attention and care of the principal and his staff. Students like this school and their teachers."

"The school serves about 900 students housed in classes of about 45 students each," Hassan explained. The curriculum, which is designed by Jordan Ministry of Education, has changed over the years. The most significant change came after the 1994 Peace Treaty with Israel. According to Hassan:

> The curriculum is now centered on human rights, children's rights, democracy, and tolerance. They have taken away the Palestinian history book. Now we teach about Arab history and Islam, geography and nature. The Palestinian story is no longer the main focus. It did not completely disappear, but it was marginalized. The Palestinian student has become part of the Arab and Islamic world.

Hassan explained that even if the curriculum is modified, it does not mean that they can't still teach the history of Palestine. "Our students are very well aware of their general and personal history. Every student, when asked, will tell you about their original village in Palestine and their desire to return home."

To demonstrate, he gave me a tour of two classrooms and introduced me to the students, asking them, "Where are you from?" All students answered by giving the name of their original Palestinian village. He commented, "This is amazing. These students and their parents have never been to Palestine, but they know the story." He continued, "Students understand the meaning of being a refugee. It is a condition of poverty, expulsion, and pain. They understand that the only way to fight these oppressive conditions is to stand up and get educated. They understand that the right of return is sacred."

The school halls were filled with Palestinian symbols including the flag, names of villages, maps, and embroidery.

A VOICE OF LOYALTY

At times, Hassan believes that he has a special mission to serve the Palestinian cause. His father was killed shortly after Hassan was born, while on his way to visit his brother in Gaza. His father and all of the other passengers on board a bus were killed by what he referred to as "Jewish terrorist groups such as Hagana and Ergun," on May 15, 1948. His mother also died in Jordan on May 15, 1995. Hassan points out that May 15th also holds significance for the history of Palestine: May 15th is the date on which Israel declared its independence. For the Palestinians, this is the official date of the *Nakba*.

Like his students, he remains loyal to his family history:

The Jewish military forced us out of our village, A'qer, next to Ramleh. They gathered all the men in the village under a tree and threatened to kill them with knives. Although the British forces stopped the planned massacre, they did not stop the expulsion of Palestinians from their homes. My mother, then a widow with five children (Hassan is the youngest), went to Al-Khalil (Hebron). We walked all the way there. We settled in Dura, Al-Khalil until 1960, when my mother decided to join her family in Jericho. We lived in a refugee camp until the war of 1967, when we were forced to move out for the second time, as refugees, to Zarqa Camp. The Israeli army attacked the camp and the Ghor region in the Jordan Valley. Consequently, all camp residents moved to Zarqa through Madaba in Jordan.

Hassan graduated from college in 1968. His mother was very poor but he has been successful, as has his brother who works as an engineer in the United States. Hassan has worked in the field of education as a school teacher for about thirty years and as a school principal for the last four years.

Hassan is very proud of his family and his Palestinian heritage. His wife is also Palestinian and they have seven children. His oldest son is a dentist; his oldest daughter is an occupational therapist. His youngest daughter is now in Third grade and his other children are college graduates working in their professional fields. He believes that resistance to expulsion and oppression is grounded in education. "My mother didn't have a penny to spare but she sent us all to school. I pass her determination on to my children and grandchildren."

As to the solution of the Palestinian-Israeli conflict, he believes that it lies in a one-state solution. He stated, "It must be (a) democratic and multi-ethnic, multi-religious state. (The) two-state solution is not a recipe for peace. As long as they continue to divide the people and the land there will be no peace. There is no substitute for the return of the Palestinians. They must be compensated for their suffering and they must be allowed to return home. We can live together with the Jewish people. We have done this in the past. Now they don't want us in our homes. That is pure racism."

Hassan continued:

We, here in Jordan, have changed our curriculum to accommodate the Peace Treaty of 1994, but Israel didn't reciprocate. Despite stability in Jordan, and despite the fact that Palestinians in Jordan feel loyal and are thankful to this country, most Palestinians want to return to their homes in Palestine. I am very loyal to Jordan, but down deep in my heart I am Palestinian. There are two things that I care most about: God up there and Palestine down here on earth. The refugee camps are the only reminder of the Palestinian tragedy. They must remain until a final solution is reached. Palestinians are not willing to receive reparations for their property, but they must be compensated for their pain, loss and suffering. Moreover; Jordan is not the alternate homeland. Although Jordan without the Palestinians could become a meaningless country and its role in regional and international affairs would diminish, and although Jordan has a special role for the Palestinians, yet most Palestinians want their original homes.

And he concluded: "As long as we have life, we have hope. As long as we have children, we have hope."

NOTES

1. Edward Said (1935–2003) was a renowned Palestinian American. He was a University Professor of English and Comparative Literature at Columbia University,

and was a founding figure in postcolonial theory. He was a scholar of international acclaim known as a literary theorist, cultural critic, political activist, and an outspoken advocate for Palestinian rights. His classic and extensive work earned him various national and international awards.

2. Some of those displaced persons my have been refugees from the *Nakbeh* of 1948. Said differently, some displaced persons may have become refugees twice. Once in 1948 and the second was in 1967.

3. Peace Treaty between Jordan and Israel, 1994. http://www.kinghussein.gov.jo/peacetreaty.html (1 June 2008).

4. "Black September" refers to the uprising between Palestinian organizations and the forces loyal to King Hussein of Jordan in September 1980, which ended in a serious defeat of Palestinian forces and the expulsion of the PLO from Jordan. See http://palestinefacts.org/pf_1967to1991_jordan_expel_plo.php (1 June 2008).

Chapter Four

Irbid Camp, February–March 2006

Irbid is the largest city in northern Jordan. Some refer to it as "the capital of the north." It is located about thirty kilometers from the Syrian border, about 120 kilomenters from Damascus, and about 20 kilometers from the northeastern Israeli border, close to Tiberius and to the Golan Heights. The historic places of Jerash, the Ajloun Castle, and Umm Qais are within the vicinity of the city of Irbid. Yarmouk University has a Center for the Study of Refugees and Displaced Persons (Center) with which I had a professional affiliation for the duration of my Fulbright research project. Yarmouk University is named after the river Yarmouk and is also known for the famous six-day battle of 636 between the Muslims and the Byzantine army, which ended in a victory for the Muslims, hence the expansion of the Muslim Empire.[1]

As I walked into the Center's office, I was greeted by a young man who introduced himself as Abedalbaset. He is a researcher at the Center majoring in economics. He accompanied me to the office next door. We sat down and chatted about the Center and the refugees. He was eager to give me information and to make me feel comfortable. Shortly thereafter, a man walked in with the traditional Arabic coffee (Qahwa Sada). Moments later Dr. Khalaf, another researcher at the Center, joined the conversation. Dr. Khalaf and Abedalbaset pointed out that the majority of Palestinian refugees in Jordan are full Jordanian citizens, and that the camps remain standing as a symbol of the *Nakba* and a reminder of the right of return. At that moment Ms. Alia, the office manager, walked in followed by Dr. Ali Zaghal. He greeted me with warm Arabic greetings of *Ahalan Wasahlan, Nuraheb Feekum* (Literally, welcome to your family and home). He invited us to his spacious, comfortable, and nicely furnished office. There I also met Ms. Manar, who works in this department and was responsible for computer-related functions.

Dr. Zaghal is a distinguished gentleman who seems to be in his late sixties. He established a well-recognized center with an international reputation and funding from a variety of sources including Oxford University, George Mason University, and others. Dr. Zaghal has the aura of a distinguished professor and is treated with utmost respect by his staff. They address him in a formal manner—the title "Dr." always precedes their comments. Although I have noticed that this is a common practice here in Jordan, it seems that with him, the staff use this term with a sense of awe and admiration.

They expressed interest in my work, shared information and provided me with a selection of their publications and other material related to the study of refugees.

A VOICE OF DISCIPLINE

Following this introductory meeting, Dr. Zaghal had a companion[2]—who requested to remain anonymous—ready to take me to Irbid refugee camp. For the purposes of this essay, I will call him Kheir. He is a young man in his early thirties and of Jordanian origin. He is not of Palestinian roots. The staff at the office arranged for us to meet with the Mukhtar in the camp. The streets were busy as we drove through the city of Irbid. The neighborhoods changed as we moved from one to the next. Some looked more affluent than others. At some point, Kheir said: "You may not be able to realize that we have entered the camp. The neighboring streets are not much different." A minute later he declared that we had entered the camp. There was no sign indicating the entrance but as we proceeded deeper inside it became clear that something was different: narrow streets; people moving aimlessly around; and children playing in the street. Women were also out in the street either walking with their children or sitting in front of little doors and small housing units. The streets, better described as alleyways, were dusty and there were no trees at all. One cannot find any type of green plants. When I commented that there wasn't any type of green plants to be found, to this my companion replied, "There is no room to plant anything."

We arrived at the door of the target office of the Mukhtar and the Improvement Committee. There was no where to park. My companion asked me to get out of the car so that he could park very close to the wall in a very narrow street across from the main entrance. "This is illegal," he said, "but I have no choice." As he made the turn I noticed a pile of garbage by the dumpster.

We went up to the third floor. The Mukhtar was sitting in his office behind a large desk. There was a young man who was introduced to us later as Mr.

Obeidat, the office secretary. The Obeidat family is one of the largest tribes in Jordan, I was told.

The Mukhtar's demeanor was official, and the pictures of the current king of Jordan, Abdullah II, and that of his father, the late King Hussein, were displayed on the wall behind him. The Mukhtar was dressed in a suit and wore the red *Kafia*[3] (headdress for men) on his head signifying a traditional Arab elder. The red color is common in Jordan. After brief greetings, he pointed out that we were expected to arrive fifteen minutes earlier. His secretary commented, "This man is so disciplined! Everything must be done on schedule and on time. Even the call of nature – He goes to the bathroom at specific times."

My companion, Kheir, continued to praise the Mukhtar as to his efficiency and accomplishments. He seems to hold much power in the camp. He is also the chair of the Improvement Committee in the camp, which, according to Kheir, has accomplished a great deal under the leadership of the Mukhtar.

Kheir did most of the talking, but I introduced myself and noted my interest in visiting the camp and meeting a family willing to share its story of refuge with me. Both the Mukhtar and his secretary responded that he, the Mukhtar, is very familiar with the Palestinian narrative since the Palestinian revolt of 1936. He added that he is from a small village near Haifa and that he still has family in Israel. He said that one of his relatives, Mahmoud Darawsheh, is a member of the Israeli parliament (The *Knesset*).

"Have you ever visited your home in Haifa?" I asked.

"No!" he said emphatically, and continued, "I'll never visit my home to see it occupied by foreigners. I'll do so only if it is liberated. My brother went to see it, but I did not."

"I noticed that you are wearing the red *Kafia*. That is a Jordanian symbol. Do you wear the black, Palestinian Kafia?" I inquired.

"You are right, I wear the red one. Many Palestinians wear this color, and many Jordanians wear the black Kafia," he said.

"But your accent is also Jordanian," I added.

"I live in Jordan, I am Jordanian. If I were to live in Palestine, I would be Palestinian," he said with no hesitation.

He was very pleasant but guarded in his answers. I noticed that whenever the king's name was mentioned, the adjective *Jalalat* (His Majesty) had to be added. The Mukhtar was very particular about that. When I once said "King Abdullah," the Mukhtar added "His Majesty." Later, on our way to the bus station, Kheir discussed this practice and noted, "If you noticed, we here in Jordan are very big on titles." He added that the Mukhtar is very well respected in Jordan and that he is often consulted by the King about matters relating to the camps. Also, when the King convenes tribal or camp leaders, the Mukhtar is always among the invited guests.

During our meeting, the Mukhtar asked me to guess his age. I said, "I must say that you look young, but if I were to guess, you must be about 75 years old."

"You are very close. I am 77 years old," he replied. "You may have guessed correctly because I had mentioned the revolts of 1936," he added. He told me that he had married three times, and was widowed by his first and second wives. Now he lives with his third wife who is twenty-two years his junior. He has nine children, three boys and six girls, all of whom are married and employed.

He went on to explain that he maintains good health because he eats properly, doesn't drink coffee, and that he eats on schedule. The Mukhtar said that he likes to eat honey but complained, "It is difficult to find pure natural honey anymore." He recalled that back in his Palestinian village near Haifa, his father found a large beehive with honey in a tree on their property. He still remembers, with sadness in his eyes, the taste, the quantity, and the quality.

On our way out, he invited us to see his board room and the large elliptically shaped desk. A large picture of the His Majesty was hanging on the wall with the words "Jordan First" written on it. Because I had noticed these words in a number of locations in Jordan, I said, "I think this is a new motto?" He agreed, "It is about a year and a half old. It is designed to promote national unity and to put national priorities in order."

A VOICE OF FRUSTRATION

As Kheir drove through the camp streets again on our way to the bus station, one section was more crowded. I was amazed how people could drive in these streets. "Have you noticed the funeral tent?" he asked me. "No. What do you mean?" I asked. He drove back, in reverse, to show me a small tent, actually a blanket-size semi-tent located between two housing units with a few plastic chairs in it. "People don't have room to welcome guests, so if there is a funeral, they build a little tent like that for people to pay their respect to the dead and his or her family."

We continued through the market street of the city of Irbid. It was also crowded with vendors and people with hardly any parking spaces. As we proceeded through my companion, Kheir, made a few observations relating to camp life and to the city of Irbid. Women hold their young children by the hand and they keep the children on the side facing the traffic. There were laws to regulate traffic and business but nobody seems to care or to respect those laws. The unemployment rate nationwide is very high, but it is much higher in the camps. This is the reason for many young men and children aimlessly

roaming the streets. A large number of people were employed by the govern-
ment, but due to economic and international changes (globalization), the new
king—His Majesty, King Abdullah—has changed the structure by encouraging private business and private investment. "It is sad that the Arabs are lazy.
They are used to working for others and waiting for a handout," he said.
Aware of his gross generalization, he added, "Some," then continued: "We
Arabs—people and countries—don't know how to invest in human capital.
There is a brilliant student here at Yarmouk University but they won't sponsor
him to continue his education which would allow him to return and serve his
people. So, he has found an American university to sponsor him. Why should
he come back?"

As he spoke, my companion was in pain. With a deep sense of frustration,
he lamented, "Look at people —refugees or not—and their faces. They are
not happy. People don't smile. They have nothing to smile about. They have
no hope."

Kheir and I drove to the DPA office in Irbid, and walked up to the third
floor. The entrance and the staircase were filthy and a foul odor emanated
from somewhere inside. "This is a public government facility. Why is it so
filthy?" I asked myself. Inside the office, we found a group of men sitting,
drinking coffee, and smoking. They greeted us and offered us coffee. After
we were acquainted, they offered their assistance if needed. "Just call us if
you need anything," they said. Again, His Majesty was looking down at us
from his picture hanging on the wall.

A VOICE OF POLITICS

As scheduled, I returned to the camp. The Mukhtar was sitting in his office
with a number of men. After the introductions and the traditional coffee, one
man volunteered to accompany me on my tour through the camp. His name
was Kasem. As we exited the office, the Mukhtar gave us his blessings and
cautioned us, "Don't talk politics with people. We talk politics only here in
my office."

Kasem was in his forties and married. He was shy and didn't want to have
his picture taken; he was also shy about his family history. His family was
from Toul Karem, in the northern part of the West Bank. He was born and
raised in Irbid Camp, but through his own efforts, he moved out. Now he lives
with his family in the city of Irbid, not far from the camp. He serves on the
Camp Improvement Committee and volunteers his time for other societies
in the camp. One such society, named "The Galilee Club," offers services to
young people and a special program for orphans.

On our tour in the crowded market, he pointed out the poor quality of food available in the camp, saying, "Can you see what they eat?" He seems to have constructed a psychological compartmentalized attitude that created a wedge between him and "those camp residents." He did not want to talk about his experience living in the camp, but was eager to discuss the fact that he was successful enough to get out of the camp. "What is the difference between those who make it out of the camp and those who do not?" I asked. He was a bit hesitant but said, "It has to do with effort, individual ability and hard work."

Kasem was also eager to talk about the Galilee Club and the Center for orphan children. He seems to invest much of his time in such activities and gains much satisfaction from his contributions. He took me on a tour of the club. It was closed at that hour but we saw the outside of the building and the playground designed for ball games. The playground is built of concrete and is enclosed within four walls. It was dirty and lacked the basic sports amenities. A few children were playing soccer. Kasem made a point to highlight that this playground is "illegal." It does not meet the standards or the minimum construction code.

We walked through the narrow and dirty streets of Irbid Camp, among the rows of gray and dusty shacks on either side of us. Entry into these small, unkempt, housing units is directly from the street. There is no sign of plant life and the grimy alleyways were made of dirt, asphalt or concrete. We approached the crowded market on the main street. Men, women and children, young and old were all packed together into this noisy, dirty place. It was disorganized, with things on top of one another. Vegetable stands, meat stands and clothing stands were all in the same space with no distance between them. The meat and chicken were right out in the open exposed to the muggy daytime air. The apples looked moldy and unclean, but people were buying and selling. "Everything here could bring some kind of a disease," said Kasem as a matter of fact. "Those old clothes and shoes were previously donated by European churches. Now this is not the case. They are sold at a charge."

VOICES OF PATIENCE

On our way through the market we talked to a number of people who told us their stories.

Omar, a man with a white complexion, blue eyes and grey beard came along, eager to talk. He was 66 years old and owned a vegetable stand. He told me that he and his family arrived as refugees in 1948 and resided in Irbid Camp. He now lives with his wife and nine children in a small housing unit of about 90 square meters. "It is not comfortable. In the winter we get together in one room to get a bit warmer," he said, and continued to describe the camp as a "waiting station." "All of us Palestinian refugees are waiting here to go back to our homes. We left our homes because we were attacked. And we want to return. Everyone here in the camp is waiting for that. We won't move anywhere but to our homes in Palestine." He still has family in Palestine (Israel), near Haifa. He has gone to visit them only once, in 1975. "Our family is scattered all over," he added.

Others were standing by. There was a young boy of 15 holding his little niece in his arms. Both were smiling. He said that he was from Haifa and that his father had passed away. His uncle is the main supporter of their family.

Khalil was 75 years old, and married to two wives with fifteen children. He said he is from the Al-Khalil (Hebron) region and his family became refugees in 1948 when the Israeli army attacked his village. (Note that Khalil is a common name in the Arab world and it refers to the city Al-Khalil (Hebron) that is considered sacred to the three Abrahamic traditions. Al-Khalil in Arabic means 'the friend' which refers to the patriarch Abraham who was known as the Friend of God).[4]

> They destroyed our village. So we moved to another village. But in 1957, after the 1956 war, the Egyptian army withdrew and told us to leave and that we would return in few days. They gave the land to Israel.

Khalil spoke with sadness and continued, "The dust of my village is better than all we have here."

Um Khalid is a 64 year-old women who had five children. Like other women, she spoke with me in public. She came to Jordan from Nazareth, Israel in 1961 to join her uncle, who was a refugee from 1948 in Irbid Camp. Her husband was disabled and remained inside their home all day long. They did not have any source of income, and are dependent on charity from UNRWA. "I don't have any hopes," she stated, adding: "My hope is either death or to live in our homeland in Palestine—even if it is in a tent."

Ahmad was 65 years old, lived with his two wives and 14 children in a housing unit of about 150 square meters. "There was some space available, so we expanded our original housing unit," he explained. He spoke briefly of his origins and the core of his beliefs.

> We fled from the area next to Nazareth in 1948. We walked for seventeen days—from Nazareth, to Lebanon, then to Irbid. Now we want to return to our homes. We wait for either death or a homeland. And we reject any form of reparations.—Taking reparations would be a sign that we are willing to sell our homes and property. It is not so.

Ja'afar, a 40 year old man, was born into a family from a small border town in Israel, where his family had owned about 360 dunham (88.96 acres) of land, before they fled in 1948. He has never visited his homeland. He lived with his 12 family members (brothers and their families) in a one-bedroom housing unit of about 50 square meters. In 1982, they built a second floor, he explained: "That was illegal, but we needed the space and we were penalized for it." He works in the field of central heating and recently was engaged. He plans to live outside the camp when he gets married. "I can't get married in this small unit. Everybody, even your neighbors, can hear every sound," he explained, his face blushing.

He led me in a tour of his house. We took off our shoes to enter. The front entrance is a small metal door that takes you into a small "living room," empty of furniture. With the exception of his father's picture, the walls were bare. There were a few mattresses on the floor. The floor was uneven—and I tripped. To enter into the rest of the house, he made sure that women were not present. We walked into a ground floor level were he keeps his business equipment. Adjacent to that space there was a small bathroom and a small kitchen that can hardly accommodate one person. I did not see a place for the shower. Hot water was boiling in the kitchen on a small kerosene-operated device called a "primus" or "Babour".

On our way out, we met Um Emad, a widow who stopped to tell us that she is originally from Smariya,[5] a small farming and fishing village to the north of Akka (Acre). She left her village and went with her family to Lebanon and later joined the rest of her husband's family in Irbid Camp. She said that old people were "stupid" for leaving their homeland. They were also scared from the atrocities committed by the Jews against the Palestinians, such as the massacre of Deir Yasin. She added that the Arab nations are not united and do not speak for their people.

For the last twenty-six years, she has lived with her family in a small housing unit with a dirt floor, which they rent for about JD40 ($56.5) per month. They receive food rations from UNRWA four times a year, and a monthly stipend of about JD38 ($54) from the Jordanian welfare system.

VOICES OF ANGER

Later in the evening, I met with Ali, the head of the Galilee Club, who was born in the camp in 1964. His family fled their home in Toul Karem in 1948; they have lived in the camp since 1950. He grew up with nine brothers and sisters and his parents in a housing unit of sixty-five to seventy square meters.

He graduated from Yarmouk University. He, too, has left the camp and now he lives with his own family in the city of Irbid.

He said his family left their home in Toul Karem because they were scared. "They were simple peasants," he stated. Expressing anger with his parents for leaving their home, he continued:

> I may understand their story, but the only excuse I can give them is the fear of rape. A violation of family honor is the most important taboo in our culture. It must not be violated under any circumstances. It is true that Ardak Ardak (Your land is your honor). They also say that your gun is your honor, but nothing comes before the family honor. You give everything up to protect your family and its honor.

On our way back to the Mukhtar's office, we found a man handling dry Arabic bread. The bread was spread all over the floor. I learned that he buys leftover bread from families in the camp, spreads it on the floor to dry, and then sells it to farmers to feed their sheep. Very interesting life cycle, I thought. As we were examining that venue two men, in their mid-thirties, stopped by and told us that they were businessmen. They buy flour from poor families—their ration from UNRWA—and sell it in their own stores. I had some aversion to these men who survive from the misery of the poor. On second thought, who does not?

A VOICE OF TIME

The next day, as scheduled, I arrived at the Mukhtar's office to hear his personal narrative. He is a perfectionist, and pointed out that he tells his story to anyone who is interested, and that many journalists, historians and writers have come his way.

> My name is Qasim Abdelmalik. I was born in 1928 in a small village called Ijzim near Haifa, Palestine. We left our home in 1948 because Israeli soldiers were shooting at us with heavy artillery. We, on the other hand, had in our possession small machine guns. There was no match. We walked all night long until we arrived to the villages of A'rah and A'rarah in the triangle region of Palestine. From there we continued to Jenine. There we met the Iraqi army that welcomed us and took us straight to Baghdad. About a year and a half later, some of us, including my father, requested to move to Jordan. Jordan is much closer to Palestine, not only in distance but also in culture. Iraqi trucks dropped us off at the Jordanian border. We waited there for three days until they received clearance from His Majesty, King Abdullah I. Based on a recommendation from a Jordanian officer, we landed in Irbid Camp.

Here in Irbid Camp, the land had nothing on it. UNRWA staff provided us with tent material. We erected our own tents right here on this site and lived in them for about two years. Large families received large tents with four pillars or studs. Small families, on the other hand, received tents with one pillar or stud. We called it "*Khazouk.*"[6]

We didn't have running water or electricity. Women got their water from central locations in the camp. All this happened in 1951. Electricity came to the camp at a later stage. Eventually, with the help of Irbid Mayor, Mr. Naeem Al-Tal, we received running water. This camp land is private property of the Al-Tal family. It is rented out to UNRWA and Jordan. The streets were mud and the school was built with mud walls. Later, people threw away their tents and began to build small mud houses. About four years ago, people were allowed to build second floor units over their original housing space. Many of the original residents of the camp have managed to build their homes outside the camp. Now a new generation lives in the camp. All camp residents are Muslims. We had one Christian family that moved out a long time ago.

Under the leadership of the Mukhtar of that time, Mr. Shafiq Abu Lubdeh, people organized and paved the school yard with asphalt. Later we paved the streets. Each family, excluding the poor, donated about five pennies, and King Hussein donated to us a sum of 5000 JD ($7065) for this project. All the streets were paved in 1966.

A VOICE OF DUAL IDENTITY

Although I (the Mukhtar) am happy here in Jordan, I miss Palestine. There we own about 30 dunham (7.4 acres) of land. Our home was settled on 4 dunham (0.99 acre). I still have the deed for that property. My father worked in farming and cattle trade. My parents had a total of seven children (three boys and four girls). Now we have only four remaining. The rest have passed away. Most of our remaining family and their children live outside the camp. The difference between those who remained in the camp and those who left the camp lies in income. All people work but income is limited. Those who don't work actually don't want to work. I live outside the camp and own a taxi company. One of my drivers is an engineer. Since he cannot find employment in his field, he is willing to accept other jobs.

Irbid Camp provides for all the necessities of life. People live in it until a solution is found. Everyone wants to return back to his home in Palestine. I know realistically that the Palestinian issue is a matter for international negotiations, which take a long time. I also know that we may not be able to return to our properties of 1948. There is some hope for some people to return to their homes occupied in 1967. I am willing to return only to my home in Ijzim—not to other places. This is not realistic, but I am not willing to return to an alternate place. We reject any other form of reparation. All (of) America's money will not do. We want our homes. In the meantime we have settled here in Jordan. We have full citizenship with all its rights, and Jordan has been good to us.

I remember the revolt of 1936. The British mandate at the time was providing ammunition to the Jewish militant groups and were depriving Palestinians of the opportunity to defend themselves. Four to five years later the revolt quieted down. At the outbreak of WWII, the British found employment for Palestinians — public work. I worked as a messenger in one of those employment camps. The supervisor was Jewish and the head manager was British.

I finished seventh grade only — against my father's wishes. He encouraged me to go on with my education, but I wanted to go out to work. At the time that we were forced into our refugee journey, I was about 20 years old. The journey was difficult. We walked all night while the Jewish groups were firing at us. They really wanted to empty the land of its people. I was afraid, of course, but that didn't matter. We had to keep going. I do regret leaving my home, but I see the Palestinians in Israel today. They live a miserable life. At least in Jordan we are free. If you do not bother the state, the state will not bother you. They leave you alone. I am very comfortable here in Jordan. I have my rights and am treated equally. I carry a Jordanian passport. Palestinian refugees in other Arab countries don't enjoy such privileges. I don't prefer to live in Israel under their oppression. I have relatives in Syria and Iraq. All want to live in Jordan. In Jordan, I feel Jordanian. Once I return home, I'll be Palestinian. Everyone here at the camp wants to return home. They want a better life but their income is limited. After all, there is not much difference between the conditions in Irbid Camp and in Irbid the city. The camp's market is a very busy street.

One thing that pains me the most is remembering the day we left our land. I remember the hardship of walking all night long. We left everything in the house. We did not even take the key with us. We all thought that we'll return home after the war was over. We were in a rush to leave. We didn't take a thing with us. Some people returned to take some of their belongings. The whole village — about 7,000 people — were left outside that night. I cannot forget that.

People left because of fear. We were afraid not only of massacres, like the one they had committed in Deir Yasin, but also the most dramatic fear was that the Jewish soldiers were raping our women. This is something we can never accept. We were willing to give our land in order to protect our women. We had the hopes that we would return to our homes soon after the war was ended, and that Israel might not exist. But later we realized that Britain was leaving everything to the Jewish people. They were setting the stage for the establishment of Israel. I am not angry. Anger doesn't do you any good with big nations. But I am hopeful. My hope is in God.

A VOICE OF HOSPITALITY

On one of my subsequent trips to Irbid Camp, I took a taxi. The taxi driver was quiet, so I asked him, "How are you today?"

"I am happy with God, but not with his human creatures," he said.

"Patience is a virtue," I replied.

"What do you have at Irbid refugee camp?" he inquired.

"I have a meeting with the Mukhtar," I responded, and asked, "Are you familiar with the camp?"

"Yes. Where is his office?" he asked.

"Near the police station. Do you know how to get there?" I asked.

"Yes."

He had a stern face and his answers were short, but I continued. "I am going to conduct an interview with him. I am doing research about the living conditions of the refugees and their stories," I explained. The more I talked the more relaxed he was. Then he began speaking, pouring out his story.

I am a refugee. My family came from a small village near Haifa. We have about 500 dunham (123.6 acres) of land left behind. My family and I lived in Al Mufti refugee camp near Irbid, but in 1985, we succeeded in building a home for ourselves outside the camp. Now we live in the city.

His name was Jamil. Once we arrived at my destination, he was so comfortable, he offered me two things: First, "Don't pay for this trip," he insisted. But I politely rejected this proposition and paid the fare. His second offer was: "Come and visit with us. I was born here in Jordan, but my mother is still with us. She is 88 years old. She would love to talk to you."

To this second, offer, I said: "I will give it a serious consideration."

So Jamil added, "I am usually home after 3:00 pm. Here is my number. Please come. We don't live that far from the hotel. Consider us your family."

At about 3:30 pm, I arrived at his home. He was all smiles. He introduced me to his wife, Zakeya, his son, Ahmad (18 years old), and his youngest daughter (11 years old). He has a total of five children; two of them are in college.

The house is relatively large. It has a number of apartments which were built for him and his brothers. All the brothers worked hard, saved their money, and built this home for their families. He studied accounting and worked in the gulf countries for a number of years, which gave him the opportunity to earn enough funds to buy the land and build this home. His wife said, "We realized that if you want to make it, you have to get out of the camp—at times even out of the country."

His mother, Hajeh Amneh, who is 88 years old, remembers her home in the Beisan (Beit Shan) region and her land. The village was "Almansi," to the south of Haifa. "I wish I can see it or smell the dirt and the trees," she commented. "We are very thankful for what we have, but all of this doesn't equate with the dirt in Palestine. That is my home."

Amneh described her family's flight from their home in Palestine to Irbid Camp: "We walked for about three days and finally got to Irbid. They gave us a tent to live under. We lived in this tent for some time until we were able to build a mud house on a lot of 64 square meters." Amneh, her son, and her daughter in-law expressed pain as they spoke about their lives in the camp:

> We didn't have running water. Women went to a central location and carried jars of water on their heads. We also did not have private bathrooms. They were public, one for men and the other for women. We remember people waiting in line. This was (a) painful, embarrassing, and shameful experience.

Jamil said that since he was born and raised in Jordan, he has a special bond to this country. "I am loyal to it as much as I am loyal to Palestine." His son Ahmad, who is a college student, was quiet for most of the time but listened attentively to the discussion. Ahmad said that he learned much about the Palestinian narrative from his family. He said that he was born in Saudi Arabia, so he has another part to his identity.

On my way out, Jamil accompanied me to the door and said, "This is your home now. There is nothing between us except what is forbidden by God."

I was speechless. This was one of the most welcoming powerful statements that I have heard from any person, anywhere on this planet. I was embarrassed by this overwhelming flow of emotions. Arab hospitality is well known the world over, but this form of it was really very, very special. It was beyond description.

NOTES

1. For more information about the battle of Yarmouk, see All in Jordan. http://www.allinjordan.com/index.php?cGc9Q2l0aWVzJmN1c3RvbWVyPUJhdHRsZStv ZitZYXJtb3Vr (4 April, 2009). Also, Medieval Sourcebook at Fordham University. http://www.fordham.edu/halsall/source/yarmuk.html (4 April, 2009).

2. A companion is a person from the local community assigned to accompany me during my field research and introduce me to others in the community.

3. *Kafia* is a traditional head cover or a scarf for men known in the Middle East. It traces its roots to pre-Islamic era and also found in traditional Jewish and Christian communities of that time. Kafias come in a variety of colors and designs. Palestinian Kafia is black, while the Jordanian is red.

4. Josef W. Meri, Jere L. Bacharach, *Medieval Islamic Civilization: An Encyclopedia of the Middle Ages* (NY: Routledge, 2006), 318.

5. I am familiar with the location of Smariya. I recall that up to the 1980s, the mosque was the only structure left standing, everything else had been leveled. On my last visit to the area in January 2006, I observed that the mosque was gone and a wide highway was built across the village. The village, Smariya, and its buildings have vanished.

6. *Khazouk* is a Turkish word that refers to a stud used to hold tents and other objects into the ground. It is said that the Ottoman authorities used the *Khazouk* as an instrument of punishment by forcing it through the rectum; hence the negative connotation of *Khazouk*.

Chapter Five

Jerash Camp, February–March 2006

I called Jamil, the taxi driver from Irbid. He was very accommodating and we drove off to Jerash Camp, also known as Gaza Camp, which is about 40 kilometers north of Amman. He took the scenic road. It was really beautiful. The mountains are magnificent and the road was delightful. As we passed through the city of Jerash, one could see the historic Roman ruins of times long past. There is so much history there. Every stone has a story to tell—so many wars and so many battles, so many deaths and so many religions. This region, along with Palestine, is full of history—it is a place where religion, politics, and land mix together and continue to create an ever-changing yet stable culture. It is a place where the past coexists with the future, and where paradoxes and contradictions continue to unfold.

As we were closer to the camp, the taxi driver stopped by a vegetable stand at the side of the road to ask for directions. The person at the stand looked very tired. He seemed to have the vigor of youth but looked old. He came closer to the taxi, looked through the window on my side and said, "Go straight to the traffic light, turn left and go straight. You'll run into the camp. Once you see buildings made of tin material, you will know that you have arrived." We followed his directions and he was right.

The roads inside the camp became very narrow and crowded and there were children in the street. The scene is now familiar to me. I am no longer shocked or surprised. I am confused. I really don't know if that is a good thing or not. Questions ran through my head as the driver again stopped to ask for directions.—Am I becoming immune to this brutal environment? Have I lost my humanity? Can one see this misery and not feel a thing?

A teenage youth came to give us directions. He was working but I couldn't see exactly what kind of work he was doing. Again his directions were accurate. The driver said that both men were camp residents.

"How do you know?" I asked.

"They knew the exact location. Also their demeanor shows it," he responded with confidence.

"What is it about their demeanor?" I was curious.

"They look *Masakeen* (very poor). They also look *Maqtoa'een* (rootless)," he responded with passion in his voice.

"You seem to understand this phenomenon," I commented.

He was quiet until we reached our destination. He offered to wait for me, but Jameela from the center for mentally retarded children and the two gentlemen seated in her office suggested that it might take some time and that they would take care of my transportation to Irbid.

VOICES OF DISPLACEMENT

Jameela is a woman in her forties. Her pleasant demeanor, mixed with much warmth, reflects a genteel and kind nature. She welcomed me into the office at the center for retarded children and introduced me to two men whom she had invited to meet with me. Both were teachers who were assigned to teach in the second shift at UNRWA local school. It must be noted that due to overcrowded schools, with 45 to 50 children per class, the schools in almost all of the camps I visited offered two school-day shifts: morning to noon; and noon to four in the afternoon. Yet, the two-shift school day at Jerash Camp was not sufficient. Therefore, they also offered what is known as *Sufouf Tayara* (flying classrooms) to accommodate those students who did not have classrooms assigned to them.

"Most of the residents here are from Gaza; they were displaced from their property after 1967 war."[1] An attempt was made by those present in the office to distinguish between a refugee and a displaced person: "Displaced people have fewer benefits," they asserted, referring to displaced persons from Gaza (See Chapter 1), and continued, "Displaced persons do not qualify for legal employment in Jordan; they are not granted work permits; they have a temporary status in Jordan and are not granted the national identification card that is given to Jordanian citizens, including other Palestinian refugees who were Jordanian citizens. In addition, they are not permitted to own more than one private vehicle. They don't get permission to drive a public automobile. Nor do they qualify for health or for welfare benefits. Also, benefits granted by UNRWA are limited. Although there is not much real difference between a

refugee and a displaced person, there is a difference in their legal status and
their eligibility for benefits."

Jameela described the conditions of refugee life at Jerash Camp:

> The camp is situated in the valley between the surrounding mountains on 750
> dunham (185.33 acres) of rented land. With about 30,000 residents, it is very
> crowded. All families live in the same size housing unit (96 square meters).
> Some families have as many as 21 persons living together. People survive from
> seasonal farm labor. They have to manage with the little they have. People are
> not allowed to own private businesses or work in the public sector. They are not
> permitted to visit the neighboring Arab countries, so they cannot even look for
> new opportunities. [Because of all the restrictions described above], people ex-
> perience pain and injustice daily and suffer from discrimination, poverty and at
> times hunger. But the sad part is that some people adapt to living with injustice.

VOICES OF ESCAPE

Kheir, one of the two teachers mentioned above, was born in 1962 in Gaza.
His family belongs to the Bedouin tribes of the Beir Sheba region of Palestine. De facto, these people became refugees twice, in both 1948 and 1967.
In both cases, the fear of atrocities and rape was the overriding force for their
decisions to leave. "I still remember the massacre of Abu Rashed," he said,
explaining:

> Jewish soldiers shot people to death in cold blood. They lined them up and shot
> them into a ditch. They planted fear in our hearts, so we escaped. There was a
> truck driver who drove my family across the river to Jordan with the few be-
> longings we had managed to salvage from our home in Gaza. Later we learned
> that this driver was cooperating with Israel—He used fear tactics to encourage
> people to leave. At the bridge, the Israeli soldiers spoke to us in broken Arabic
> and in a sarcastic tone, they said: 'wheen Raich ya khabibi— Hussain? Rooch,'
> which translates to 'Where are you going, my dear/love? To Hussain? Go
> ahead.' They opened the gate wide open with a big smile on their faces.

Speaking with despair Kheir continued:

> Once we crossed the Jordan River, the UN staff gave us a tent—everyone re-
> ceived a tent: a white tent for small size family and a green tent for a large size
> family. Families were given choices as to their destination— they were free to
> choose their camp location. People's decisions were based on family unity. Our
> family settled in this camp, Jerash. We call it "Gaza," because most people here
> are from that region. Here in the camp we received food, blankets and basic

necessities from UNRWA. There was no water—a truck would pass by from which women filled their jars. When we arrived in February of 1968, it was cold, with snow and rain every day. We didn't have water to take a shower, and we didn't have private bathrooms. There were only public facilities. People had to wait in line. It was miserable.

Every family received a 69-square-meter (743-square-foot) lot. With time, people started building small units made of asbestos. Some people had their housing conditions improve a bit, but most continue to live in such terrible environment. Ninety-nine percent of camp residents are not Jordanian citizens; because they are from Gaza they hold the temporary resident status. They have large families—the average family size is 7.5.

While Kheir, Jameela and Saif, the other teacher in the room, debated the average family size—some claimed it is 8— they also explained the reasons, despite poverty, for having large families. In fact, Saif, a man in his forties had a total of thirteen children. "There are a number of factors at play," Kheir stated.

This is a religious, political, and social matter. The religious point of view is obvious—You have your children and God will take care of them. The political dimension has to do with demography. People want to keep the demographic edge over Israel. And as to the social factor, having many children is *Ozwa*, power and social prestige.

VOICES OF STRENGTH

Kheir continued to explain that people in Jerash Camp have very strong ties. They help each other out when needed. As Kheir explained, the rest nodded with agreement:

As Bedouins, we have strong loyalty to the tribe. We were nomadic tribes, and our loyalty was to the tribe, not as much to the land. Our family honor is primary. One cannot retrieve his honor if it is lost, but one can certainly retrieve his land. Land comes next on our list of priorities. Also, nobody has the right to remove us from our homes. That decision is for us to make.

According to a report on "Forced Displacement of Bedouins, an Ethnic Cleansing!"[2], the presence of Bedouins in Palestine is centuries old. Most reside in the Naqab (Negev) region with small communities in the outskirts of Jerusalem, in Haifa district and in the Galilee. Their manner of living combines a settlement and nomadic style, and most of them work in agriculture

or pastoral labor. The report also states that the Bedouins have always been
and continue to be targeted by Israel for their land.

Jameela was born in 1963 in Anssairat refugee camp in Gaza Strip. Her
family fled their property in Beir Al Sabea' (Beir Sheba) and became refugees. They escaped during the 1948 war because of torture and other atrocities against the Palestinians. Her family, like that of Kheir, is of Palestinian
Bedouin origin. She recalled that in Gaza, Palestinian refugees encountered
discrimination from the Gazan natives. "I used to hear statements like 'A
donkey's face is the same as that of a refugee'," she said, and added, "Following the 1967 war, we witnessed the Jewish soldiers burying young men
alive." Her father left to Egypt and never returned. Jameela, and her mother
and her three sisters were cared for by relatives, and ultimately landed in
Jerash Camp.

> We have been here since 1968. My mother was the one who raised us. She
> worked hard laboring on farms here in the area. We suffered as orphans, as
> displaced people, and from poverty.

Jameela was educated in UNRWA schools. She attended college and
earned a BA degree in business administration. She is married, has four children, and lives with her entire family in one of the standard, 96-square-meter
housing units. "People say that I am like Condoleezza Rice because I am a
strong woman," she said with a smile.

I boarded a local car on my way back to Irbid. The driver was a camp resident. Once on the road in his van, he told me that he once conducted surveys
for fund raising purposes for a charity organization. Once they discovered
that he was a displaced person, they let him go. He could not get any other
job, so he used his van as a transportation vehicle. He was not permitted to
collect money because that would be considered "public transportation," but
he adds, "I have to survive."

VOICES OF MISERY

For my next visit to Jerash Camp, I took the bus marked "Jerash–Gaza Camp"
from Abdali bus station in Amman. People were boarding and taking their
seats.—There is no need to purchase a ticket ahead of time, one just enters
and takes an available seat. When about twenty passengers have boarded the
mini-bus, its driver would get on board and collect the fair before hitting the
road.

The seats were very small. There was another passenger next to me, and half of my body was hanging off the seat; it was uncomfortable. The passengers were quiet; their faces looked sad. A little boy was trying to make some fun but people didn't smile. Their faces and their shoulders were down. As we were closer to the camp, most people were getting off. I asked the driver if Jearsh camp was on his route. His answer was somewhat rude, "Aren't you going there?" and he turned away from me. A passenger next to me gave me an assuring response for which I was thankful.

At the final stop, I asked the driver for directions to Jameela's office. This time he was polite and cooperative. A passenger on the bus heard my question and offered to assist me. We got off the bus together. I told him I needed to stop at a shop to purchase a pen. He kindly offered me his pen. He told me that he works for the school and that he is related to Mr. Kheir. As we walked together up the street, I noticed an open tunnel with water flowing through it. I did not inquire but left that matter for a later time. As we walked through the school yard Mr. Kheir came out to greet me and we proceeded to the office.

On our way up the street we met an elderly man, Abu Ahmad, sitting in front of his home. He invited us into his living room. By then I had learned that the living room is the one closest to the street.

The room was empty and bare. The walls were not painted. The door leading into the rest of the house was constantly swinging. At some point, Abu Ahmad decided to hold the door closed with a plastic chair behind it. The only furniture in the room was a small round, plastic table and about six plastic chairs.

Kheir wiped his chair off with a napkin before he sat on it. Nothing in that room was clean. Abu Ahmad offered us Arabic coffee. He inquired about permits to verify if I had an official permission to be in the camp. Kheir assured him of that and I showed him a copy of my permit from the DPA.

"I am not going to talk politics," he said and began to tell his story. He was born in 1927 in Gaza, served in the Egyptian army, and found that most people were not honest. "Palestinians are the most honest and decent people," he declared. He was the only one from his family to flee his home in 1965. He talked about the Hagana group, a Jewish terrorist organization in the 1940s and the harm it had caused to the Palestinians. He regrets leaving his homeland and is ready to return. He said that since the 1993 Oslo Agreement between Israel and the Palestinian Authority, he has had his luggage packed—ready to return home at any time. "Regrets and anger don't help," he said.

During the conversation he used specific names of Egyptian soldiers and described how the Palestinians were always placed on the front line. He said that he now lives with his seventy-year-old wife, and that they have a total of sixty members in their family (including grandchildren and great-grand-children). He worked for thirty years as a guard at the kindergarten across the street. Abu Ahmad and his wife need medical attention but they don't have medical insurance and they cannot afford treatment.

In the background I heard voices of women and children. He was curious as to whether Americans were aware of "our misery." He described a refugee as one "without rights, without home, and without leadership. It is like being a fish in the sea. It keeps moving aimlessly."

VOICES OF HOMELESSNESS

On our way up the street Kheir told me that the water flowing through those open tunnels in the middle of the street is sewage water—water from showers and washing, but not bathroom water. Nevertheless the odor was strong. Later he repeated that the odor in the summer is very strong and that clean water at times gets mixed with this polluted water. People become sick but they cannot afford medical treatment. As we toured the camp later in the day with the *Mukhtar*, the odor was even stronger. Children were hanging around

Photo 5.1.   An open sewage tunnel goes through the streets of Jerash Camp, 2006.

the tunnels. It is a scene that defies description. Children look very sad. They have no place to go and they hardly have a place to play. Some children were doing hard labor, digging in the street and doing construction work. Other children were just sitting with sad faces with nothing to do, nowhere to go, and nothing to play with. Time passes by.

Back in the office with Jameela, Kheir talked more about the problems facing the camp. He serves on the Improvement Committee which is made of eleven members: all men and all appointed by the DPA. His list of the problems included: open sewage water; crowded and poor housing; no space between neighbors; high unemployment among the young (most people work in the summer- seasonal farming labor); lack of funds for improvement; poverty and lack of medical serevices.

At the center for mentally retarded children for example, the staff members are "volunteers." "We cannot call it a salary," Kheir explained, "because people are not allowed to hold a job and salaries require additional commitments, such as medical insurance, retirement funds, and so forth. So we give people charity donations—that is their salary."

At that moment, a bearded man in his late fifties walked in. He was dressed in a very traditional Arabic style with white *kafeya* (head dress). He greeted us and was introduced as the *Mukhtar* of the camp. The *Mukhtar* was born in 1950 in Khan Younes refugee camp in Gaza Strip. His parents fled their home and property in 1948 from Beir Al Sabea' located in the Naqeb region (Negev) and left behind about 600 dunham (148.3 acres) of land. He stated that in 1994, he went back to see their land: "It was pointed out to me. The Israelis use it now for two objectives: a grape farm and a military installation." He continued:

> Our families were poor and simple. They were afraid of the organized Jewish military and terror groups. And they were told that the whole 'thing' should take a couple of weeks—that everyone would soon return home. That was what the Egyptian army told us.

He added that in 1968, his family fled again because, "We saw the atrocities committed by Israel against young Palestinians. We moved from Khan Younes to Jericho, and from there to this camp."

The *Mukhtar* is married and has ten children, seven boys and three girls. He was open and candid about the conditions in the camp, describing poverty beyond imagination. People live on incomes that range from 20 to 100 JD per month. (This is equivalent to $30 to $150) "Some people are so very poor they end up eating donkey meat." He added that "Many, if not all, educated people cannot find employment. Children see that and become discouraged. Education becomes meaningless. Moreover, rats are part of the scene. They live inside and outside the homes. They enter the sewage tunnels and eat people's chicken and tomatoes and the like." He described refugees as being homeless:

> Because we are considered *Nazeheen* (displaced people), we don't have permanent residency. We are barred from employment and from other transactions. Our options are limited to summer or seasonal farming jobs.

> We are the children of Diaspora—we all have hopes to return home. When granted the opportunity all of us will stand in line to return to our homeland. Being stateless is being homeless. But we do have hope.

"I don't mean to talk politics," he concluded, "but with all the difficulties we are very thankful to Jordan. Jordan has accepted us and treated us, refugees, much better than other countries in the region."

It was lunch time. They offered to take me out to a restaurant. They rejected my offer to carry the cost – they felt insulted. The *Mukhtar* replied:

> We might be poor, but we still have our honor. You are our guest. In our tradition, a guest becomes a member of the family after he stays with the family for three days.

We laughed at this exchange—and I thought to myself, "If all they have left is their honor, how dare I challenge that."

VOICES OF DESPAIR

The *Mukhtar* drove his truck onto the highway outside of Jerash Camp to a restaurant where his son works as a waiter. Jameela was invited but she declined on the grounds that she had to take care of business in the office. As we passed through the camp, I observed that women were dressed in long black garbs, that trees and plants were nowhere to be seen, and that children and young people were out on the streets. Their faces were sad. One could hardly see a smile. Children sat quietly at the corner, seemingly frozen in space and time. No laughter, no sound, and no movement—only empty faces and hollow stares. There were also a few donkeys standing nearby.

The *Mukhtar's* brother, the principal of the camp school, joined us for lunch. He spoke with frustration as he described educational prospects for students in the camp.

> We have a total of 1,200 students up to tenth grade. Students look around and observe that education doesn't lead to anything. The dropout rate is very high. No more than 100 of the 1200 students are likely to continue their education.

As to the removal of Palestine's history from the curriculum, he was abrupt:

We teach what we are given! Decisions about the Middle East and about everything in our lives are made outside the region and out of people's hands. We don't have any kind of control and we have no say in the matter.

The discussion that followed was general, but they asked me, "Are Americans aware of our misery? Can you speak the truth? Don't they mask the truth about us?"

The next day I called Jameela to thank her and asked her to give thanks to everyone on my behalf. She was very kind and said, "Here, we live on hope—Hope is the essence of our lives."

NOTES

1. Refugees from Gaza are classified in Jordan as displaced persons from Gaza. They differ from displaced people from the West Bank in that West Bank refugee, also referred to as displaced persons, were Jordanian citizens before the 1967 war, while those from Gaza were not citizens of Jordan. Consequently, their residency status is temporary and their benefits are minimal, if any. See chapter 1.

2. Applied Research Institute in Jerusalem (ARIJ). Forced Displacement of Bedouins, an Ethnic Cleansing! 10, January, 2008,http://www.poica.org/editor/case_studies/view.php?recordID=1424 (18-May-2009). Report was prepared by Land Research Center.

Chapter Six

Al Hussein Camp, April 2006

Al Hussein Camp was established in 1952. It is located about three kilometers from the center of Amman. Actually, it is one of Amman's neighborhoods. It sits in the valley of Jabel Hussein (Jabel is Arabic for mountain). Jabel Hussein is a very active business district with many stores and little malls buzzing with economic activity. The market street is located on the mountain, while the camp is located in the valley. To get to the camp one has to drive or walk down the mountain. The streets leading to the camp are an extension of the city streets. One can't tell the difference until they are deep inside the camp. The internal streets are very narrow, crowded and dirty. The buildings are also different. Inside the camp, the buildings are small, crowded, and stacked on top of each other. Another mountain can be seen from the other side of the camp. So the camp is located literally down in the bottom of the valley. I cannot imagine what it is like in the winter when water flows down from all directions.

The camp follows administratively the governorate of Amman, which might place it in a better position to receive municipal services. It is located on about 445 dunham (110 acres) of land and is occupied by more than 30,000 residents. Most of the camp dwellers came from Lud, Ramleh, and other Palestinian villages in the vicinity of Jaffa. Families were allotted housing units of about 100 square meters each. Over the years, those families have succeeded to build more solid structures, and with the increase in population, were also permitted to build expansions on top of the first units.

A VOICE OF EXILE

I spoke briefly with Um Eyad, who is in charge of the embroidery project and educational programs at the Women's Center. She is a widow in her fifties and a mother of six. Two of her children are now married; the rest work and attend college. Her parents became refugees in 1948, coming from a village near Jaffa. She was born in Al Hussein Camp, but moved to Saudi Arabia, where she worked as a school teacher. She returned to the camp about seventeen years ago and continues to teach. "Many children now need additional tutoring, so we, here at the center, offer tutoring and other training programs to the youth," she said. She explained that schools no longer provide good education because classes are crowded with fifty to sixty children.[1] As a result, "Both teachers and students don't really care. There is a high dropout rate and the children are left behind."

Following her return to the camp, she noticed that it had changed in many ways.

There is an improvement in housing. There is more space because people were granted permits, and many were able to build expansions to their housing units.

Families in this camp don't have as many children as their parents did. My daughter has only two children, while I had six.

People keep to themselves. There is little sense of community or solidarity. Everyone is to himself. That was not the case in the past.

Many of the original residents of the camp have moved out to the city and left the unit to their children, or in some cases they rent it out to newcomers such as Iraqi refugees.

Um Eyad, who is a refugee and a Jordanian citizen, encouraged me to go down to the Camp Street, but commented,

We are filled with regrets. Life in your homeland gives you dignity. Life as a refugee is a life of exile (*musharadeen*). It lacks dignity and honor. This camp is [an] overcrowded place. It has about 38,000 residents. It is noisy, dirty and lacks privacy. Everyone wants to return to her/his home in Palestine, and we should be compensated for the misery of expulsion and exile but we should also return to our homes. No one would accept reparations or compensation for property.

The camp has a little over fifty short streets. The main street, Camp Street, divides the camp in half and serves as the camp market street. This street, unlike other streets I saw in other camps, is wide enough for two cars to pass through. Stores and vegetable stands are lined up on both sides of the street. Because products here are less expensive, shoppers from neighboring areas also come to this market—some arrive in their Mercedes to do their shopping and leave.

As I walked around, it felt as if all of the camp residents were out on the street. Lack of fresh air, the odor and the noise induced a sensation of suffocation. But for the first time in all of my visits to the camps, I saw a number of trees and a few plants. There was a small nursery. Perhaps there was life after all.

Walking up to Jabel Hussein business district, I met three little children on their way out of the camp. They asked about my camera, and I asked about their destination. They said that they were going to the playground. Here I heard words—*nursery, playground*—that I did not hear in other camps. So what made the difference? The fact that there is a playground on the outskirts of the camp may suggest that proximity to a relatively prosperous city and being administratively under its jurisdiction provide the camp with added resources and a greater sense of inclusion in public space. Yet, listening to Um Eyad, one gets the impression that economic prosperity may not erase the feelings of exile, dispossession, and the pain of injustice. For her, Palestine is home.

NOTE

1. Increase in school population is most likely a consequence of an increase in birth rates. High student population density is associated with high school population, limited number of classrooms and limited facilities.

Chapter Seven

Hitteen Camp, March–April 2006

I met Hussein in Zarqa Camp and he offered to introduce me to Hitteen Camp, his place of birth. As we were walking down the street in Hitteen Camp on our way to the Jordanian Women's Center, we met three men sitting in a little store. He introduced two of them as active in the youth club. "They try to help the youth from getting into trouble," he said. All three talked about their separation from their homeland, Palestine, and about their experience with discrimination here in Jordan. During the short time we spent at the store, they shared their frustration and despair:

> In case you are pulled over by the police, they will search and question you for no reason. Also, employment opportunities are not distributed equally. People of Jordanian origin are given better opportunities. Many say we are not to talk about politics and not to complain, so we are here stuck in nowhere. Nobody seems to care about our conditions. A tent in Palestine is better than living as a refugee. We won't leave the camp until a resolution is found. Getting reparations is a sign that we have sold our land and dignity.

We continued on our way. The streets were narrow and housing units were made of a tin material. Roofs were covered with tin plates held down by stones and bricks. The streets were dirty. The area is dusty, and people, young and old, were roaming the street. We also met little children who were supposed to be in school. I asked one little boy about his school attendance. He said that he goes to school in the second shift; that is, at noon. Yet he was on the street at that hour in the morning rather than being at home.

I thought that after having visited a number of camps my shock would subside. Such was not the case. The misery and the humiliation of the refugees are visible and shocking. I continued to wonder how the people who live in

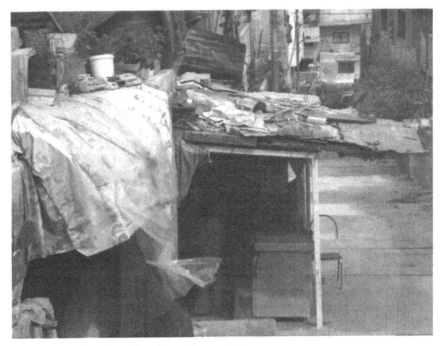

Photo 7.1.   A housing unit, Hitteen Camp, 2006.

the camp have made it this far under these conditions. I was shocked when I saw garbage piled up right in the center of the camp waiting to be picked up. A strong, nauseating odor filled the air. Hussein told me, "I didn't want to tell you about this, I left it as a surprise." And a surprise it was. Across the way I noticed a little grocery store. A little boy came out from the alley nearby. A few meters from there I saw a cat holding a piece of meat. Hussein said that this cat most likely got this meat from one of the houses nearby, pointing out that families may not have refrigerators and that their houses have many cracks where rodents and cats can get in and out easily. "That family will be left without dinner tonight," he commented. This was a scene never to be forgotten. The garbage, the cat, the store and the little boy—they all stood there in the center of the camp with a sense of abandonment. What did Hussein want me to make out of this "surprise"? I thought to myself. I did not ask him, but the message was clear: Refugees are treated as Nobodies, and no one actually cares about them.

We walked into the Hitteen Women's Center where we met the director. She was a young woman in her mid-thirties, dressed in a traditional religious outfit with a head scarf. She was pleasant, smiled softly and spoke eloquently.

Although the office was busy with a steady stream of clients, we had an opportunity for a brief discussion.

Two of her visitors were attorneys. They were curious about my project and sat in for more discussion. One attorney came to submit her application for a part-time assignment at the center. The other attorney was a product of the camp. He was born and raised in the camp and continues to live there. He pointed out that the desire and motivation for education and academic advancement among the youngsters in camp is not as high as it was in past years. Both attorneys attributed this decline to economic changes and the ongoing war in Iraq that started with the first Gulf War. They believe that the influx of Iraqi refugees to Jordan has caused a serious competition with Palestinians. They also believe that education does not lead to employment as it did in the past. Refugee camps are witnessing a high number of unemployed young men.

The female attorney noted that income was also limited and that women these days have better opportunities than men. Her explanation lies in the fact that women were more likely to accept lower wages, they were more compliant, and they were not responsible for raising a family. She added, "I make about JD 400 a month, which is not a lot. I have to use this income to cover my office and other expenses and fees, so at the end, not much is left. Yet I don't feel much pressure because the male has the ultimate responsibility for providing for the family."

Hussein and I departed and walked into more narrow streets between dusty-looking houses. We went on our way to meet Samia from the Jordanian Women's Center. Down the road, we met two men in their seventies and a little girl sitting together in front of a house. (Keep in mind that the front of the house is the street.)

We greeted them in traditional Arabic manner: *Assalamu Alaikum*. (Peace be upon you). They invited us in and we sat for few minutes on little stools. The man sitting next to me was eighty-four years old and had hearing and vision problems. As a refugee of the 1948 war, he first moved from Gaza to Hebron; and following the war of 1967, to Hitteen camp in Jordan. Yet he spoke of returning.

> Should the opportunity be there, all of us will return to Palestine. All the money in the world won't be good enough for Palestine. We are waiting. God is the only one who can solve this problem.

On our way out, one man asked if I could make a financial contribution for his sick son at home. I was truly surprised as it was unexpected. Yet, it was a humbling encounter that underscored the ongoing misery of the refugees.

VOICES OF PROTEST

Samia was pleasant and very welcoming. She was dressed in a modern style and did not cover her hair. With a big smile she opened the door. She was born in Hitteen Camp. Her family is from the Nablus region in the West Bank. She was very eager to tell us about the projects that they carry out both within the camp and outside the camp. They offer services that range from training, to general education, to nursery schools. She pointed out that having the word *Jordanian* as part of the organization's name raises questions among the refugees. She explained, "We tell them that these projects are sponsored in part by the Ministry of the Interior and are designed to help women across the Kingdom," and added, "We also offer services to the whole family, including men, but men don't participate."

In the course of our discussion, two young women who work at the Center stopped by at the end of their shift to say goodbye, but they decided to join in on the discussion. Both were in their mid-twenties; one was married and a mother of a three-year-old child. Their parents became refugees twice in their lifetime: once after the 1948 war, and again after the 1967 war. For these young women who were born in Hitteen Camp, "refugees are people who are dispersed and lost without rights." Having experienced neither war, they challenged their family history.

> People say that they (our parents/grandparents) left because of wars. We don't see any rational reason for leaving their homeland. They tell us that they left their homes and property for their safety and the security of their families, and because they wanted to protect their women from rape.

The latter was an argument they did not accept, declaring:

> Women can protect themselves. Our parents should not have left their homeland because of that reason. They (men) should have faith in their women and in God. They claim that it was family honor. That doesn't make any sense. Homeland is more important than family honor.

They asserted with anger, *Ardak Ardak* (Your land is your honor)—and explained:

> Well, it is really our grandparents who did this move. They were simple people. We always question our parents about leaving their home and property. We tell them that wars happen all the time, and if you were to die, so what? Many Palestinians didn't leave. Are we better off? No! We live in miserable conditions. They said they wanted to bring us to safety. Now we live in misery and still have no safety. So which is better?

They continued: "Refugees have neither a home nor rights. We are not safe here. The police can invade our homes and privacy at any time. We saw that (with) our eyes." One of them added, "They attacked my brother so many times because he advocated for the Palestinian cause. I saw him being beaten and injured. They would take him away (and) we wouldn't find him for months."

"So, if the conditions in the camp are so terrible, why do you stay in it?" I asked.

Their tone shifted as they spoke of their life within Hitteen Camp:

It is lack of money. But money is not everything. The camp reminds us of Palestine. We know some people who left the camp and now regret it. Here you smell Palestine. There is the comfort and warmth that a community can offer. You cannot find this outside the camp. Here people know each other and they feel comfortable with each other. One is a stranger outside the camp. The camp is our only reminder of the tragedy. Despite its difficult conditions, it has produced leaders in all areas. We have artists, lawyers, doctors and many other professionals. Hardship is the root of creativity.

And they added, "We always talk about Palestine. We teach our children about it, and we remind them of how the world has denied us our basic right to return home."

They concluded by asking:

Do you know the poem by the Arabic poet Ahmed Shawqi, Amir al- Sho'araa' (The Prince of Poets)?[1] It says:

بلادي وان جارت علي عزيزة

وقومي وان ضنوا علي كرام

[My nation remains dear to me even if it was far away, and my people remain honorable even if they oppressed me.]

VOICES OF RETURN

Five women, Khadija, Salmeh, Um Waheed, Um Kheir, and Um Emad, came to the Jordanian Women's Center to meet with me.

Khadija is a sixty-year- old mother of ten children. Her husband was in his seventies and owns a little grocery store in the camp. She talked about her family leaving their village of Salmeh in the Jaffa district in 1948. Her oldest brother insisted that because of the war, in order to protect their women, the family must leave. She did not want to leave, but her brother and her father forced her to do so: "I actually ran back home, but they came after me. They were concerned with Jewish soldiers raping their women." They moved out, as did everyone else in the village: "Everybody was leaving – the whole village. They were so afraid that they left everything behind." They "settled" in Balata, a refugee camp around Nablus in the West Bank, where they remained until the 1967 war. Following that war they moved again to the east side of the Jordan River and settled in Amman. She moved to Hitteen Camp when she married and moved in with her husband. Because her husband is a refugee from Gaza, he and their children do not have citizenship rights in Jordan and do not qualify for many UNRWA services. They are required to renew their visa documents every two years, which is very costly: "The fees add up to a lot of money which we don't have. It costs JD100 for an adult and JD20 for a child. We can't afford it."

"I want to go back to Palestine. It is my right to return home," she asserted, and continued:

> We don't want compensation for our land. We want to return home. I dream of it all the time. I want to go back home and plant my vegetables and live off our land. Life in Balata Camp was much better than living in Hitteen Camp. Here we live in a housing unit of 80 square meters. We have no place to plant anything. It is so dry.

Um Waheed was about seventy years old and a mother of nine children. Her family moved from Ajour, a village near Al Khalil (Hebron). She recalls that the Jewish soldiers moved into the village:

> There was an Egyptian commander at the time that encouraged people to leave. He told us, 'You'll come back home once the war is over.' Later we discovered that there was a land broker who wanted to sell our land to the Jewish people. He, too, told us to leave and come back after the war.

She recalled riding on a camel and crossing the Jordan River. They settled in Karameh, Jordan, until Israel attacked Karameh in 1968, and a new war started.[2] So they moved again. "Wars force us to move. We moved every time there was war," she said. With tears in her eyes, she also spoke of her dream of returning:

> My mother told us everything about our land and about life in Palestine. I dream of our home and property in Palestine. I dream of the fresh air and the olives of Palestine. I'd go back any time, even if I can't walk, I'll go back crawling on my knees.

Um Kheir was a forty-seven-year-old mother of nine children. "We have many children," she says, "to be of help to the family and to keep the cause of Palestine alive." Her roots go back to Deir Nahhas, near Al Khalil, from where her family moved following the 1948 war. They settled in Jericho where they worked as farmers in Jordan across the Jordan River. Following the 1967 war, Israel closed the borders and prevented them from returning to Jericho; so they were placed in Baqa' Camp. She described the miserable life she had in Baqa' Camp:

> We lived in a tent where water was running underneath our feet. We had to find cement blocks and wood to raise the floor. We used to walk in muddy roads. The tent leaked all the time, and we did not have private bathrooms. There were public facilities—one bathroom for each section of the camp—that was used by both males and females. Women and young girls used to wait until late in the afternoon to use that bathroom. This was so painful and so embarrassing. The bathroom had a hole in the ground. That is all. For water, we walked two to three kilometers to a central location and bring water back home. To get enough water, we had to wake up very early in the morning, about 4:00 am, to be the first in line. Oh! those were miserable years. We didn't have space or privacy.

With her determination, Um Kheir graduated from high school. At the age of eighteen, she accepted a teaching position in Saudi Arabia, where she worked for a total of five years. Following that experience, she came back to Baqa'a Camp, married her husband (who was from Hitteen Camp), and has lived in Hitteen Camp ever since. She describes daily struggles for survival—small space, lack of privacy, a leaky roof, and low income. Her husband was sick and unemployed; they barely had enough to eat. Yet, she looks at life in the camp as a temporary arrangement: "The camp is a reminder of the *Nakba*," she said, and believed that one day they would return to Palestine. She concluded, "A homeland means independence. Palestine is for Palestinians."

While all the women I spoke with had only their hair covered, Um Emad, on the other hand was dressed in black robe and covered from head to toe. She wore the Burqa (a face cover that allows only for her eyes to be visible). She was a woman in her early thirties and a mother of five children. Her husband was a Bedouin from Beir Al-Sabea'. He was unemployed and was ineligible for citizenship. Her roots go to Toul Karem in the West Bank. Because her family was active in the liberation movement, they moved to Kuwait after the 1967 war. She was born and raised in Kuwait. In the late 1980s, she moved with her husband to Zarqa in Jordan. "Kuwait doesn't provide retirement packages, but life in Zarqa was too expensive for us; so we moved to Hitteen Camp where we have resided for more than eleven years now," she said, adding that she had visited Palestine at the age of eight and that her family still holds, as proof of ownership, a deed to their land in Palestine. They want to return home, but "It is very difficult to fight the Zionist policy," she concluded.

VOICES OF HOPE

Escorted by Hussein, I walked through a small door to go down below street level to get to the "guest room" in a family's home. We took our shoes off and walked into a small room with mattresses placed around the walls and an old carpet on the floor. We sat on those mattresses and were greeted by a number of women.

Um Riad was very active in the meeting and was very enthusiastic for the opportunity to have a discussion of this kind. "We can always learn something," she stated. She was a forty-year- old mother of five children. "We used to have many children because people didn't have satellite TV," she said jokingly. Her family came from Barj Ibn Amer, near Haifa. They were told that they would return—that it would not be long before they could return home. She continued at length:

> Our parents were afraid of gunfire. It is (a) fight or flight kind of situation. They could not fight. They also wanted to protect their women. People were poor and simple at the time. They valued family honor over their land. Today they feel guilty and we feel angry with their decision.

Hussein interjected, "Family honor and land honor are equally important. How could you choose between your two eyes?"

They were quiet for a moment, and then Um Riad continued:

> (Being) a refugee means lack of stability to us. It is like drowning. A camp is like a temporary arrangement. People go on camping trips and will eventually return home. That is our status. Refugee camp life is not pleasant. Our status as a refugee is like that of a pregnant woman—she will have pain to the end, but the pain will go away once the baby is born. We are here because we suffered and are looking for safety. Palestinians are lost. They experience pressure from all sides. They are not united and lack leadership. They lost their priorities. Even the Palestinian Authority seems to have forgotten the real cause. The Jewish people always affiliate with the strongest nation. Palestinians always lose.

> We believe in God. People lead an empty life. Religion equals nation. We must restore our faith in God, and that is how we can put our priorities back in order.

People, young and old, have a strong attachment to Palestine. We love Palestine, and that is hope. While most people live in their own countries, for us, Palestine lives in our hearts.

The other women present nodded with agreement.

A VOICE OF LAMENT

Um Khalid, an eighty-four-year old widow, had finished her prayers and joined us half-way through the discussion. She sat quietly until she was asked about her experience of the *Nakbah* of 1948 when she was in her early twenties. She recalled, "Jewish soldiers shooting at us and at our village, Sajad, near Lud and Ramleh," and added:

As they were shooting at us, we moved to the field, but they followed us and continued shooting; so we moved to the next village. We continued to move until we arrived in Jericho.

Although everyone did that, I did not want to leave, but my husband forced me to join him. He told me, 'The Jewish soldiers will rape you.' On the road I noticed that we had no food to eat, so while they were moving away from home, I ran back on my donkey and got the chicken to feed the children.

We all were told that we would be allowed to return home at the end of the war. So my grandfather buried three jars of gold out in the yard, and we left with our cows, camel and donkey. When we arrived in Jericho, UNRWA gave us a tent. We stayed there until 1967 war, when the Israeli soldiers were shooting at us again. So we moved for the second time. They assigned us to Wihdat Camp, then to Irbid Camp, and finally to Hitteen Camp.

Tired by her forced "nomadic" life, she lamented:

I don't want to move again. I don't even want to return home. At the moment I don't own anything in Palestine. Here in the camp, I know that at least I have a home.

NOTES

1. Ahmed Shawqi (1868-1932) is known as Amir al- Sho'araa' (literally, the Prince of Poets). http://www.nationmaster.com/encyclopedia/Ahmed-Shawqi (29-Dec-2008). The poem quoted here refers to the love of the poet for his nation. It is

transcribed as "Beladi wa in jarat a'layya a'zeezatun wa ahli wa in dhalou a'layya kiraamo" and translated to English by the author.

2. "The Battle of Karameh, 1968," *Washington Report on Middle East Affairs* (March 1998): 87-88. http://www.wrmea.com/backissues/0398/9803087.html (8 August 2008).

Chapter Eight

Baqa'a Camp, April 2006

I met Ziad at the University of Jordan after I had returned from a conference in Jerusalem. Ziad, who works as a messenger, inquired about the conference and added, "I wish I could visit Jerusalem."

"Have you ever been to Jerusalem?" I asked.

"No, we are from Nablus."

"So, I take it you were born in Jordan?"

"Yes, we are considered *Nazeheen* (displaced persons) of 1967."

"What is the difference between displaced persons and refugees?"[1] I inquired.

"Displaced persons supposedly were removed from their Palestinian property after 1967, while refugees of 1948 were forced to leave. They have different legal status: refugees hold a white UNRWA card and receive benefits from UNRWA, while displaced persons hold a yellow card and don't qualify for benefits," Ziad explained.

"But I also understand that displaced persons don't qualify for residency in Jordan. They hold temporary status. They cannot acquire a 'national number.'"

"This is true only for the displaced people from Gaza." he said.

"What is the difference?" I asked.

"I really don't know. They divide us Palestinians into so many groups. What is the difference between *Nazeh* and refugee anyway? We all have been displaced and dispossessed from our land and home. We all suffer from similar conditions," he stated with anger, and continued, "Sometimes I ask my parents, why did you leave your home? Is it not better to die in your home than to live in a refugee camp?"

A VOICE OF INJUSTICE

As he became more reflective, Ziad spoke of living conditions in Baqa'a Camp:

> We live in Baqa'a refugee camp. You should go there, Doctor. It has a bad reputation. There are so many people living there on a small piece of land. There is high unemployment among the young and the crime rate is also high. We suffer from discrimination because we are Palestinian refugees and because we live in Baqa'a. We suffer from double trouble.

Although I never visited Baqa'a Camp, I learned from the publications of the Department of Palestinian Affairs (DPA)[2] that Baqa'a Camp was established in 1968, following the 1967 war, on about 1,436 dunham (354.8 acres) of land. It is located about 20 kilometers north of Amman. It has a population of about 90,000 people, the majority of whom are from Ajjour, Beit Mahseer, Al Jaftelek, Faloujeh, Beir Sheba, Abbasiya, Jericho, Someil, and other Palestinian villages. The camp has a total of 7,100 housing units, the average size of which is 100 square meters.

Ziad was a thirty-nine-year old man with high school education. His wife, who was twenty-seven years old, is a refugee from Irbid Camp. They have two boys: Mohammad, five-years old and Ahmad, two-years old. They live together with other siblings and their families in the same housing unit in Baqa'a Camp. His father was sixty-seven years old and retired from his position as a messenger at the University of Jordan . His mother was sixty years old. His parents had ten children—five boys and five girls. Ziad is the second oldest. His older brother also works at the University of Jordan in a similar position as Ziad's.

Reflecting on Ziad's words and tone of resignation, I asked, "What type of discrimination?"

"If you want to marry, people tell you, 'You live in Baqa'a.' If you look for a job, people put an "X" on you because you live in Baqa'a."

"So why don't people leave the camp?" I asked.

"They cannot afford to," he replied, explaining:

> Their average income is about JD120 per month. Some, only a few, make more than JD500. Things are very expensive out there. I started out here in this position as a messenger for JD120 a month. Now I make about JD155 a month. Once you take taxes and other deductions out, I bring home about JD135. This is nothing. We have to survive however. So, instead of eating meat daily, we eat meat once every other day.

"Can you save for your future?" I asked.

He laughed with embarrassment and said, "No, I can't save! It is impossible." With a deep sense of frustration, he continued: "Some people make more money for the same position because they have *Wasta* (connections). *Wasta* is big here in Jordan."

A VOICE OF RESISTANCE

Although Ziad has never seen it, he has a strong attachment to his family's land in Palestine. He said that Palestinians will never accept reparation for their property because it will appear as if they had sold their land "by choice." He continued, "That will never happen, because the land was taken away from me by force. I wish I could go back home. Anything there is better than being a refugee."

I gave Ziad a piece of paper with a circle on it (Identity circle) and asked him to divide this circle into slices according to his sense of attachment or loyalty to each of the following dimensions: Arab, Palestinian, Jordanian, and Muslim. Ziad was cooperative and marked fifty percent of the circle as Muslim. He divided the other half equally between being an Arab and a Palestinian. Ziad said he feels the Jordanian part is "meaningless" and that he would encourage his family and friends, if a just and equitable solution is reached, to return to Palestine. "Jordan is a place of residence but not a home," he proclaimed. However he concluded, "Some, not many, but a few people may accept an alternate solution or settlement – they may sell their property and accept Jordan as their homeland."

NOTES

1. See chapter 1.
2. Hashemite Kingdom of Jordan, Department of Palestinian Affairs, *55 Years in Serving Refugee Camps*, 2003.

Part Four

SHARED MEANINGS
AND IDENTITIES

Chapter Nine

Farewell

The time arrived. Four months after I started my interviews, conversations and discussions with refugees, it was time to close my project and to say goodbye. Saying goodbye is not only the right thing to do, but also makes sense from the research point of view. It provides closure for both the researcher and the community. It gives those members who contributed to the project a sense of accomplishment that their time, effort, and cooperation were indeed important.

Saying goodbye to those in official positions was easy. Those who hold official titles seem a bit comfortable. For them there is continuity. Their bureaucratic positions grant them a sense of contribution and power. But for the refugees, the story was different. Separation means distance, end, and finality. But an end could also mean a new beginning.

Our relationship over those short four months was close and open. People were cooperative. They trusted me and opened their hearts and minds, and in some cases they also opened their homes. Their expectations were simple. Or, were they? All they wanted was to deliver their voices and to tell of their tragedy—to let the world know of their misery and pain and that they are waiting for an end to it. Not any end, but a just one—as they see it.

Hussein, my companion, from Hitteen Camp was tense and disappointed and talked about lack of hope. He pointed out that the camp had not had water for a week now. Jordan is mostly a desert terrain where water is scarce. Families in Amman, for example, have built wells on their properties to store water upon delivery. The frequency of water delivery varies by region or neighborhood. Hussein told me that refugee camps receive water twice a week. So it is possible for families to run out of water. But this time, the situation is rather different. Hussein stated:

We were told that something is broken and it would take another week or more to have it repaired. So people are running out of water. Those who have some money may have water delivered to their homes. The rest will have to suffer. Ultimately, they will have to buy water but they will suffer financially.

Everything was dry and the environment looked depressed. People looked tired and sad. Smiles were hard to come by. On our way to the highway, Hussein talked about "moving out." Later I realized that he was talking about emigration. "I have relatives in the U.S. and in Germany. I may go to Germany. There is no future for us here," he concluded.

Some refugees, like Samiha from Zarqa camp, pointed out that Jordan continues to emphasize a "Jordan First" policy, declaring that Palestinian refugees should not be receiving any special services. "They don't want to listen to us. They don't want to recognize that camps constitute a special case." Most did not see any bright future. Although all of the interviewees spoke of their desire to return to their homeland, some, like the two attorneys from Hitteen camp, have recognized that refugees may never return home and "The youth are lost—the younger generation has lost hope, vision, and direction."

Abu Ahmad from Jerash Camp said at the time of leave taking:

> I don't want to talk politics, but I feel comfortable with you. There is not much hope here. In God's name, I tell you that I have my luggage ready to return home. You cannot trust anybody here. They have been talking about repairing the sewage system for the last five years, but nothing has happened.

Then with despair and frustration, reflecting the fact that promises are not kept, he declared: "They all are liars!"

As I reflect, I note that field research is done from the perspective of the community. It is their voices, ideas, dreams, and visions that get recorded. In this context, field research offers an opportunity for empowerment. Yet in the case of Palestinian refugees in general or of camp residents, despair seems to be more powerful than any light of hope that might come out of a simple research project. Hope was difficult to find. In fact, their expectations are that things will get worse.

As I returned to my comfortable middle class suburban town in New Jersey, I left the refugees behind in their own pain. I left with a heavy heart.

Chapter Ten

Themes of Palestinian Identity

The voices of the refugees were purposely recorded in full to give the reader a clear sense of reality on the ground and to listen to their narrative. Camp life is much different from all that is familiar. As Hussein from Hitteen Camp pointed out describing the conflicting conditions, the misery and the ongoing pain of Palestinian refugees, "We live in a reality that is not reality". This chapter centers on some important themes that have emerged from those interviews which shed some light on the Palestinian identity in general and refugees in particular.

Before we venture into these matters, we will take a look at a brief quantitative summary of those interviews. Table 10.1 provides a presentation of some characteristics of the interviewees. Those numbers do not include interviews with officials at the various departments, including the Department of Palestinian Affairs (DPA) and the United Nations Relief and Works Agency (UNRWA).

The figures in this table point out that a total of 43 interviews were carried out. One interviewee was of a male of Jordanian origin who is married to a Palestinian woman. The other 42 individuals were all of Palestinian ancestry. The interviewees included twenty-three (23) males (53%), and 20 females (47%). Forty-four percent (44%)—19/43 of the interviews—were first-generation refugees; 51% (22/43) second-generation; and the remaining 5% (2/43), third-generation refugees. The majority, 67% of the interviewees, resided in the camps. The remaining 33% were former camp residents who had moved out of the camps.

Table 10.1.   Interviewees by camp, gender, place of residence and generation of
refugeehood

Camp	Total	Gender		Residence		Generation		
		Male	Female	In Camp	Out Camp	1st	2nd	3rd
Zarqa	10	6	4	3	7	2	8	
Irbid	11	7	4	5	6	5	6	
Jerash	5	4	1	5		5		
Hitteen	15	5	10	14	1	7	6	2
Al Hussein	1		1	1			1	
Baqa'	1	1		1			1	
Total	43	23	20	29	14	19	22	2
	(100%)	(53%)	(47%)	(67%)	(33%)	(44%)	(51%)	(5%)

FORCED REMOVAL: VIOLATION OF LAND,
FAMILY HONOR, AND THE RIGHT OF RETURN

The refugees who spoke with me were passionate about their narrative and persistent in their outlook on the history of the *Nakbeh* and its consequences. They talked about the misery of living in refugee camps and the pain of being poor and stateless. They yearn for the "good old days" and demand that they be allowed to return home. The stories of the majority of interviewees sounded similar. They were emphatic about their Palestinian *Asl* (roots) and expect to return home to their original Palestine. They imagined their villages to be in the same order they were before the *Nakbek*, and talked about planting their vegetables and eating olives and honey. Above all, they expressed a feeling of dismay and apprehension about the fact that the world community in general and the United States in particular, seem to have neglected them and ignored their just cause.

The refugees talked with much pain about dispossession from their homeland. All—both men and women—also felt deceived by the parties to the conflict, and in so many words they pointed out that at the time of the *Nakbeh*, Palestinians were not responsible for the wars, were attacked for no fault of their own, and were told to leave for a few weeks before they would be allowed to return home. Everything was supposed to be temporary—the camps, UNRWA, and the rest. The refugees share a profound sense that they were innocent victims and were ready to return home immediately after the war of 1948. But promises were not kept and their right of return was denied. Instead, Palestinian refugees have been left behind in miserable conditions for more than sixty years. Yet, most of those who participated in this study were determined to stay put and wait for a just solution. As Hassan and others asserted, "Our right of return is sacred!" They believe they have moral and legal ground for this right. Those claims are supported by historical and legal research as highlighted in the work of Michael Kagan[1] who stated that:

> Historical research has generally backed up Palestinian claims that they were expelled from their homes by violence and fear, and likely by a systematic campaign of ethnic cleansing. Legal research has illustrated that the right of return has broad roots in international law.

During the interviews, it became obvious that the causes for leaving their homeland recounted by Palestinian refugees fall into two categories: forced removal, and fear. Both causes are equally important and neither can be denied. In talking with men and women in the camps, it became obvious that in addition to forced removal, the other forces that propelled many refugees to leave their homeland can be summed up in two issues: fear of harm to family members from military attacks and fear of losing family honor.

Loss of family honor is a significant ancient tribal taboo in most human cultures.[2] Family honor is one of the most important cultural codes of the community. It refers to both the role of men to provide for and protect their families and property and to the notion that sexual purity must be protected and observed—that sexuality must be expressed only in the proper marital context. Consequently, according to culturally defined gender roles, women ought to be protected from external invasion and rape. Any invasion or violation of such norms, or even the threat of such violations, poses a danger to family honor and dignity.

For many Palestinian refugees that were interviewed, this fear of losing family honor was justified. According to historians such as Ilan Pappe[3] and Benny Morris[4], the war of 1948 included numerous cases of rape of Palestinian women in a number of Palestinian villages and towns such as Acre, Ramle, Jibalya neighborhood and Deir Yasin. The Israeli historian, Benny Morris makes it rather obvious that rape and the fear of rape have played a significant role in the flight of Palestinians from their homes. He goes on to report details of some of those cases including that, "On 14 or 15 of May, a 12 year old girl was raped by two Haganah soldiers. There were also a number of attempted rapes." (P. 220).

The interviews made it obvious that this fear has gender and generational dimension. No one disputed the facts that rape took place and that the fear of rape was real. Men that I spoke with, regardless of generation, considered rape a serious violation of family honor and that they, men, were responsible for protecting their women. This sentiment was echoed by the first generation of women refugees as well. But the younger generation—third generation refugees like the two young women from Hitteen Camp—challenged that notion and asserted that this argument did not make any sense to them. They were disappointed in their grandparents for making such decisions "as if women can't protect themselves," they complained.

In addition, a second important honor was also violated: the honor of the land. Palestinians claim that *Ardak A'rdak* (Your land is your honor). Land is treated as a sacred entity that ought to be protected. In a patriarchal agricultural society, such as that of the Palestinians of the *Nakbeh* era, men were placed in a position that required them to protect both honors—women and land. It is not a mere coincidence that for Palestinians, the Arabic term *Ard* (land) is a feminine word representing the female gender that is the source of life and creation—a mother to be sure.

In traditional Palestinian culture, land and women symbolize life, creation and survival. Both land and women are considered vulnerable entities that could be at risk of being invaded and violated. Hence, placing men in a position of responsibility to defend and protect both is of paramount importance. A choice between these two sacred entities is not an option. As Hussein, the young man from Hitteen Camp put it, "How could you choose between your two eyes?" Nonetheless, during the *Nakbeh* male Palestinian refugees found themselves in a situation where they felt forced to make such a choice. Such a decision was justified by Kheir from Jerash Camp explaining that one can recover his land but not his family honor. Whatever justification may be out there, that decision was a traumatic experience of loss that is linked with guilt, shame and anger. The second and third generation refugees seem to understand that their parents and grandparents had faced a complex and challenging reality, but they—the women more than the men that were interviewed—tend to question their elders' decisions. Speaking in a group of women in Hitteen Camp, Um Riad pointed out that their parents could not fight to protect the land, but they escaped to protect their women. In her judgment, "people were poor and simple at the time. They valued family honor over their land. Today they feel guilty and we feel angry with their decision."

At the time of the *Nakbeh,* although both men and women interviewees were equally anxious about the survival of their family members, the men were concerned with matters of fight, flight and personal safety, whereas women were concerned with matters of nurture and nourishment. The story of Um Khalid, an eighty-four-year-old woman, is a poignant example. She found herself compelled to return home under fire "to get chicken for the children to eat."

These divergent views and conflicting perspectives demonstrate the confusion that is prevalent in the camps and points out that the tendency for self-blame is likely to be correlated with their helplessness. The decision to leave was the result of force and/or fear. It was not a matter of rational choice. When victims of war blame themselves for their loss, depression and hopelessness may set in, as stated by Jamal from Zarqa Camp: "Nobody cares about our cause. We all will die here in our misery."

Yet there is convergence over the sacredness of land, family honor and the right of return. Palestinian refugees have totally lost confidence that political institutions will work in their favor. The traumatic loss of their existential foundation has left a mark in their core being. In the absence of all worldly hopes, it is difficult for the observer to ignore the intensity of the refugees' belief that God is the ultimate savior.

ALIENATION IN FOREIGN LAND: CAMPS AND PALESTINE

Palestinian refugees in the camps I visited live in Jordan but they don't consider it their home. They feel alienated in a "foreign" land and they reject the idea of *Tawteen* (settlement in Jordan as an alternative nation). Some of the refugees were granted Jordanian citizenship; others, particularly those from Gaza, were not. Some are classified as refugees, others as displaced persons. But do these formal classifications really make a difference? In addressing this question, Ziad from Baqa'a Camp explained, ". . . they divide us Palestinians into so many groups. What is the difference between *Nazeh* (displaced person) and *refugee* anyway? We all have been displaced from our land and home. We all suffer from similar conditions," he stated with anger, and continued: "Sometimes I ask my parents why they left their home. Is it not better to die in your home than to live in a refugee camp?"

In general, it seems that those with Jordanian citizenship have better opportunities in terms of employment and movement than those who don't. Nevertheless living in the camp seems to trump other factors. Citizens or not, camp residents suffer the most. They experience discrimination, higher rates of unemployment, poverty, high infant mortality rates[5], poor health, poor quality education, meager housing conditions, domestic violence, and more. They seem to reside in a prison-like environment.

So, how do those refugees cope with such conditions of alienation, poverty, misery, statelessness, and gross neglect? And how do they negotiate their identity? But the most obvious question still is what prevents them from leaving the camps. If the conditions are so terrible, why do they stay? Why don't they leave?

To address these questions, we will look at a number of cultural and political factors that have shaped the identity of those refugees. Since politics and culture are interconnected, and since political matters are addressed through cultural behavioral patterns, the discussion to follow deals with both factors simultaneously.

The *Nakbeh* and its aftermath have, for the last sixty years, limited the identity spheres of the refugees and created a vacuum between their reality on the ground and their perceived identity. While they dream and think of Palestine, they don't live in Palestine. Coping with such conditions requires creativity and much symbolism. That is precisely what refugees have at their disposal. Creative symbolic ideas are critical tools for finding a meaning in their everyday struggle.

As they search for meaning in their lives, they find themselves neglected by the international community. Meaning is also associated with respect. Their questions as to whether Americans understand or care about them reflect their hunger for recognition and respect. Robert W. Fuller[6] reminds us that the hunger for social and public appreciation is one of the deepest and most profound attributes of the human experience and that recognition deprivation may drive people to violence and unreason. Fuller's articulate argument may find a home in the Palestinians' experience. Their personal and cultural trauma have led to their sense of invisibility which serves as a prominent attribute of those who are classified as "Nobodies" He points out that Nobody wants to be a Nobody, and that "Nobodies" are ignored, silenced and disconnected.

Under these harsh conditions, where do they find optimism? Both men and women were optimistic about the future, but each perspective was derived from different roots. Men like Hassan from Zarqa, and Kheir from Jerash Camp pointed out that as long as there are children, there is hope. Some claimed that as long as they believe in God, there is hope. But Um Riad, a second generation refugee female from Hitteen Camp claimed emphatically, "Refugee camp life is not pleasant. The situation of a refugee is like that of a pregnant woman—she will have pain to the end, but the pain will go away once the baby is born." And the two young women from Hitteen Camp spoke of the "warmth of the camp community" as a metaphor for the mother's womb. Refugee camps then stand as a symbol of injustice that is yet to be rectified. More than that, Palestinian refugee camps serve to remind Palestinians and non-Palestinians alike of Palestine, and that people should not forget their *Asl*—their roots. Yet, above all, camps also stand out, regardless of their harsh reality, as a warm place for Palestinians to be together. In short, the camps keep Palestine alive. "Hardship is the root of creativity," claimed those two young women from Hitteen, noting that this is what gives the refugees hope. They do believe that this harsh reality will ultimately bridge the gap between their dreams and reality and produce the real Palestine for them. In the meantime they will try to stay warm while waiting in the cold.

LOVE FOR PALESTINE

When asked to introduce themselves, Palestinians generally mention their Palestinian village or town of origin. Whether they were born in Palestine or not, and whether or not they have ever been to Palestine, regardless of how many generations removed, and regardless of their place or country of residence, Palestinians always mention that they are Palestinians and point to their original village or town. The children in the school I visited in Zarqa Camp were no exception. When asked, they all responded by stating their ancestors' villages in Palestine. Um Riad from Hitteen Camp made the point very clear. "Most people live in their own countries; for us, Palestine lives in our hearts," she declared with a smile on her face. Palestine to them is well and alive and its story is passed on from one generation to the next. Whether the schools teach it or not, parents and grandparents do.

The refugees' love for Palestine is unwavering. It is firm, persistent, and strong. It is also spiritual. Ziad from Baqa'a Camp and a number of others from Irbid Camp made it obvious that they feel it is better to die in one's homeland than to be a refugee. The spiritual connection to the land is so strong that some name their children after Palestinian landmarks as was the case of the little girl named A'kka. Matters of life and death are strongly associated with their love for Palestine. Hassan, the school principal from Zarqa Camp, made his devotion very obvious. He declared: "There are two things that I care most about: God up there and Palestine down here on Earth."

And there are those with dual identities. Ibrahim from Zarqa Camp pointed out that first and second generation refugees speak in Palestinian accent that is typical of their region, but their children are changing now—they speak with a Palestinian-Jordanian accent that, according to him, creates confusion and loss. Compared with alienation, duality might be a function of a greater degree of assimilation. While it might appear pragmatic, it has the potential to reinforce marginality. The Mukhtar from Irbid Camp represents a classic case of duality. He is a first generation refugee who seems to enjoy high prestige in the community, and is rewarded by the King of Jordan. He wears the red Jordanian *Kafia* or *Hatta* and speaks with a Jordanian accent. During my interview with him he declared without much hesitation that, "I live in Jordan, I am Jordanian; if I were to live in Palestine I would be Palestinian." For him there was no ambiguity. The matter is clear cut. Identity is flexible and changeable depending on the circumstances. Yet, he lives outside the camp.

So does residency make a difference? Keep in mind that being Palestinian is at the core of all interviewees' being. However, those who live outside the camp have adopted a perspective different from that of camp residents. They move between the Palestinian and Jordanian spheres with greater ease. They are pragmatic and try to make miserable camp life better. These are the school teachers, the health workers, the UNRWA workers, and the social service workers. The school principal is religiously passionate about his Palestinian identity and lives outside the camp as well.

During my visit with the improvement committee in Zarqa, the head of that committee, who is of Jordanian ancestry and never lived in the camp, stated as a matter of fact, "Refugees have dual identity." The rest of those seated in the room, all of Palestinian origin remained quiet. They did not challenge or support this notion. Still, their silence spoke volumes. I could not exactly read their reaction. Could it be that because they hold formal positions on the committee, they are required to go along with the "official line" as declared by a Jordanian man who serves as their head; or perhaps they were afraid to speak their mind in front of their Jordanian director, or perhaps they were confused? Whatever the case might have been, their ambiguous position propelled Zein, who served as my companion on that day, to point out their hypocrisy and to declare that, "They are all crooks."

And yet, there is another factor: place of employment. One could argue that a refugee's identity may vary depending on the interaction between residency and place of employment. A closer look at such interactions suggests that refugees address their reality differently depending on their place of residence and place of employment.

One group is made up of those who reside and work in the camps – which represents the majority of those who were interviewed. They are very passionate and identify themselves as Palestinians. They are emotionally expressive and have a strong attachment to their original Palestinian villages.

The second group includes those who reside in the camp and work outside the camp. The brief interview with a young male lawyer from Hitteen Camp who happened to be present at the Women's Center with his colleague, a female attorney, serves as an example. While he lives in the camp and works both in and outside the camp, she lives and works outside the camp, but was interested in a position at the Center in the camp. The male attorney was much more concerned about the younger generation and their identification with the Palestinian Cause, while the female attorney was concerned about her economic well-being.

A third group of interviewees are those who reside outside the camp and work in the camp. This category refers to a number of individuals mentioned earlier: the Mukhtar, Kasem and Ali from Irbid, Ibrahim, the school principal, and the women from the Women's Center in Zarqa Camp. Members of this group share two important features: they have very strong feelings for Palestine while trying to be pragmatic. They want to help the refugees at the humanitarian level. They are very aware of reality and are busy trying to do something about it. They want to bring more resources and more attention to the camps; they want Jordan and UNRWA to provide more and better care. Most of them believe that the camps should be improved but not demolished. These people know how to negotiate the system and to serve as a bridge between the refugees in the camps and the system.

Fourth, there are those who both reside and work outside the camp. The female attorney mentioned above fits this category. It is important though to keep in mind that Jordan is home to a large segment of Palestinians, many of whom are refugees but have never lived in refugee camps. They are part of mainstream Jordan. They are highly assimilated and many of them have achieved economic success. Some of them are university professors, medical doctors, business owners and the like. I met a number of them during my stay in Jordan, but consistent with my focus on camp populations, I did not interview them and did not include them in my research. There is also the family of Hajeh Amneh, her son, Jamil and her daughter in-law, along with her grandchildren from Irbid City. They succeeded to leave and to get out of the camp and build a place for themselves. The mother, Amneh, a first-generation refugee, was very emotional talking about Palestine. For her, "The dirt of Palestine is better than all they have here." Her son, Jamil, a second-generation refugee, made the point that he was born in Jordan, therefore he is Jordanian, but he can never forget his Palestinian *Asl*—roots. His son, a third-generation refugee stated very quietly that he was born in Saudi Arabia, which makes his identity much more complex. In the face of so much complexity, Jamil was a very generous host. "This is your home now. There is nothing between us except what is forbidden by God," he told me as I was standing by the door on my way out of his house. Hospitality is a well known Arabic tradition, but in the context of identity, it symbolizes connection to a wider community of Palestinians. Hospitality is also part of their identity.

There is still another category that stands independent of the rest: Jerash refugees. They stand alone, almost totally disconnected from the outside world. They differ from most other refugees in a number of ways. They are not Jordanian citizens. In fact they are not citizens of any country. They are from the Southern part of historic Palestine—Beir Al Sabea and Gaza—and are classified as *Nazeheen*, displaced persons. Their employment opportunities are severely restricted, as is their movement. They live in a de facto prison, but they seem to maintain close and strong tribal ties. They help each other out and as Jameela stated, "Here we live on hope." But a number of them asserted, "We have our luggage packed and ready to return to our Palestinian home."

The numerous patterns and themes that emerged from those interviews highlight the fact that Palestinian identity remains strong, but it has become multifaceted and more complex. This observation makes the link between identity and community spheres rather obvious. Refugees who live and work in the camps, including those from Jerash Camp, have very limited and close circles. Most of those around them are Palestinians. Their interactions with outsiders are minimal at best. While at the same time, those who live or work outside the camp are more likely to expand their community spheres with the outside world. Hence they face a reality that requires them to negotiate different forms of identity that range from the professional, pragmatic identity (bridge people) to the dual national identity (the Mukhtar from Irbid Camp).

Above all these similarities and differences, the refugees I spoke with couldn't hide their love for Palestine. For them, Palestine is both: a physical place and an idea which remains, as it has always been, a place they call home.

NOTES

1. Michael Kagan, "Do Israeli Rights Conflict With the Palestinian Right of Return? Identifying the Possible Legal Arguments," *BADIL* Resource Center for Palestinian Residency & Refugee Rights (August 2005): *Working Paper* no. 10. http://www.badil.org/al-majdal/2005/Autumn/article7.htm (29-Dec-2008)

2. See, for example, an Old Testament perspective, Deuteronomy 22:20-21. (*Holy Bible–New International Version*) International Bible Society, 1984. http://www.biblegateway.com/passage/?search=Deuteronomy%2022:13-21;&version=31 (31 May 2008). Although most Palestinians are Muslims, it is important to note that Islam and Judaism, as well as Christianity, are rooted in the *Abrahamic traditions*. These three monotheistic religions all evolved from the ancient tribal culture of the Middle East. The point here is that the notion of family honor predates Islam and is derived from pre-Islamic traditions.

3. Ilan Pappe, *The Ethnic Cleansing of Palestine* (Oxford, England: Oneworld Publications Limited, 2006), 90, 132, 156, 176, 184, 208-11.

4. Benny Morris, *The Birth of the Palestinian Refugee Problem Revisited.* (NY: Cambridge University Press; 2 edition, 2004), 220, 231, 257, 301.

5. The Palestinian refugee infant mortality rate in Jordan in 2000, according to UNRWA, was 32 per 1000 live births. This rate is considered one of the highest in the region. See http://www.un.org/unrwa/publications/pdf/figures.pdf (26 August 2008).

6. Robert W. Fuller. *Somebodies and Nobodies: Overcoming the Abuse of Rank* (British Colombia, Canada: New Society Publishers, 2004).

Chapter Eleven

Thwarted Dreams and Arrested Development

The twentieth century witnessed many tragedies including World War I, World War II, the Holocaust, the Palestinian *Nakbeh*, the Armenian Genocide, the Bosnian Genocide, and far too many others. Events of such magnitude serve as a critical point in history, as they divide parties to the conflict into winners and losers, and time into before and after. Victory brings celebration, rewards, control over resources, and recognition. More importantly, it brings about a new order and establishes a new power structure. While the winners exert efforts to maintain their gains and to perpetuate their hold on power and resources, the losers occupy an imposed status that is almost devoid of personal choices, becoming increasingly invisible and preoccupied with restoration of justice.

This extraordinary interaction is woven into a multifaceted web of racism, discrimination, stereotypes and, ultimately, oppression—which comes in a variety of forms: economic, religious, cultural, and political, to name only a few. This is precisely the case of the Palestinian refugees. Alienation has become a fixed feature of their experience. Their oppression is multidimensional: they are poor, stateless, isolated, and invisible. Power disparity in any social structure imposes a subordinate status upon the weaker party in the conflict. According to Dodson, "A group has power when it has the capacity to make its interests felt as an impact in communal decision making."[1] In the end, the opinions and aspirations of the weaker group in the larger geopolitical context are deemed irrelevant. It begs the question therefore, whether the existence of a subordinate party may be a necessary requirement for the survival and success of those in power. This suggests that subordinate parties are expected to accept their destiny and to participate in the evolving process but not to determine its outcome. Their voices must not be heard—they are to remain "invisible."

As power disparity persists, the identity of the weak party is likely to be oppressed. Samah Jabr,[2] a young Palestinian women and practicing psychiatrist, who lives under Israeli occupation, is aware of how "power flows away from the occupied and toward the occupiers," leaving the oppressed empty and obedient shadows. She warns her fellow Palestinians not to succumb to those tactics. "The last thing we want for our people is resignation," she asserts.

In *The Souls of Black Folk*, W. E. B. DuBois pointed out that "dual heritage" or "double consciousness"[3] is a critical factor in determining the identity of oppressed groups, thus suggesting that identity formation is a function of both structural conditions and individual choice. While the structure limits individuals and defines their worldview, they still aspire to freedom. For Palestinian refugees, freedom is closely linked with the time before the *Nakbeh*—that is, freedom is defined as restoration of the structure existing before the 1948 war. Consequently they have resigned themselves to a waiting status with a fixed view on their tragedy. Fixation on a suppressed past or ideals is closely linked with dreams deferred. Martin Luther King's dream was an example of such dreams deferred, where a large segment of the African-American community and other American minority groups are awaiting the fulfillment of the promises inherent in that dream. Dreams alone, though critical to building a vision and setting goals, are not actions. Dreams deferred, without organized mobilization, can render beholders—particularly those under oppressive structures—passive.

What has become increasingly obvious from my interviews with Palestinian refugees in Jordan is that both the structure and the people are desperate. Living in a dream and waiting in a deprived, oppressed environment have tragic consequences: anger, frustration, guilt, shame and at times aggression. Some refugees face domestic violence, others resort to alcohol, and most resort to religious rituals as a symbol of solidarity, salvation, and hope. The refugees seem to be trapped in a cycle of despair. Personal progress can only be achieved outside the camp, yet leaving the camp has the potential of diluting their national identity. Not only is leaving the camp an expensive undertaking that most can't afford; leaving the camp may also imply giving up on the dream and the quest for justice. Yet the mere existence of Palestinian refugees poses a challenge to the status quo and to the existing power structure: their presence constantly reminds others of injustice done to them and demands that it be rectified.

During my visit with Zein from Zarqa Camp, his little daughter insisted that I take pictures of her birds placed in a cage hanging from the ceiling. The image was profound. The birds, confined inside the cage, stood as a reminder of life in the camp, and symbolized their desire for freedom. Looking at a bird in a cage—one sees the bird but not its total being. The cage's wires always

Photo 11.1. Bird in Cage, Zarqa Camp, 2006.

tend to obscure the bird's whole identity. They mask the view, and serve as a systematic structure that makes it impossible for the bird to fly away—to be free and fully expressed.

Palestinian refugees live in a prison-like environment, yet many of the people I interviewed seem determined to stay put and wait for a just solution. This is the paradox that refugees find themselves in. On one hand they occupy and hold an involuntary imposed status, while on the other, they search for hope. Having large families might provide a vivid illustration of this point. Given the limited resources and the very crowded nature of the camps, one would expect smaller families, but that is not the case. Instead, many of those camp residents have large families. Keeping in mind that the infant mortality rate of Palestinian refugees in Jordan is one of the highest in the region,[4] and that there is a positive correlation between family size and the infant mortality rate,[5] some of the refugees I spoke with pointed out that having many children serves some of their essential social, economic, and political needs. They argued that children serve three important functions. First, although modern, technologically advanced societies consider children an economic burden and a liability to the family, in traditional agricultural societies they serve as an economic asset. Children have the potential to add to the economic well-being of the family. Second, children in traditional and agricultural societies of the Middle East are a source of social power and pride (*Ozwa* is Arabic for power, strength; *Oz* in Hebrew) for the family. Third, children are a source of national strength. That is to say, refugees may have lost their political power, but they find power in the most intimate institutions—marriage and family. Their mere existence as Palestinians is their power and a source of hope.

Here again we witness how oppressive structures limit people's choices and bring the human character to its basic fundamental level, which in turn stand as a hindrance to its progress. Having many children is a metaphor of the farmer's agricultural mind at work: planting seeds is the number one activity with the potential to give hope for survival and salvation. The higher the number of seeds planted, the better the chances for growth. But—and this is a big but—Palestinian refugees are no longer farmers. They dream of returning to their farms, while living in a camp that is totally different from any farm. This paradox between dreams and reality give rise to two potentially contradictory results: hope and despair.

These conflicting forces, along with limited resources, and a prison-like environment, have produced a number of personal and existential problems, a sense of political impotence, and arrested development. Palestinian refugees have resided in those isolated disconnected camps for sixty years now with the bare minimum needed for survival. They lack the infrastructure that could enrich their personal and cultural lives, and are largely dependent on the humanitarian aid of UNRWA and charity organizations for their survival.

Dr. Younes, a medical doctor who lives in an upper middle class neighborhood in Amman, and is a survivor of Deir Yassin massacre[6] put it this way: "I have always felt that my life as a Palestinian had ended on April 9, 1948." Things are frozen in time and place. Although he has achieved much progress at the personal level, his Palestinian identity and culture seem to have been halted or lost, thus making his whole identity incomplete. Given that culture and society are not synonymous terms, it is essential to point out that while culture is the soul of society, society is the structure that maintains that soul and perpetuates its institutions. Cultural survival and progress are dependent on solid social institutions. The destruction of the Palestinian farming society and the fragmentation of its people make it difficult for Palestinians to preserve and advance their own culture.

Palestinians in general, and camp-resident refugees in particular, have been removed from the power structure altogether and have been deprived of possibilities for progress. Their emotional attachment to the land and their heightened awareness of their Palestinian roots and identity, are coupled with a political reality that has prevented them from fulfilling their dreams, and continues to do so. This, along with a strong sense of injustice that has not been rectified or acknowledged, characterizes their imposed status and causes a lag in their progress. While others were moving forward, Palestinian refugees were left behind—waiting.

We have come full circle now to argue that the imposed status of refugeehood is responsible for the formation of both conflicted identity and arrested development. Yet, regardless of the changes that are sweeping the region, the camps remain untouched. With all their troubles and misery, the camps are part of the social and political landscape that amplifies the refugees' feelings of dispossession and alienation. These "human warehouses"[7] stand as a symbolic reminder that the Palestinian struggle has not ended. In a dry, hot, dusty landscape, empty of plants and animal life, the camps are a reminder to the world and Palestinians alike of the cruelty of injustice. "Improve the camps," most say, but "don't remove them." Some have also added, "We shall remain here until a just solution is reached. It is the warmth of the community that makes the camps a very special waiting place."

Something strange happens to the human spirit when it suffers from injustice. When injustice is not rectified, the spirit is injured. When justice is not served, injustice becomes a very powerful moving force. It is obvious then, that for the purpose of serving the interest of hegemonic powers of dominant groups and their states, poor nations and stateless populations turn into objects to be dominated, manipulated, and abused. Palestinian refugees have equated, to a large extent, the act of rape and family honor with the loss of land. A number of refugees and non-refugees, Palestinians and Jordanians alike, have said in so many ways that Palestinians in general, and refugees in particular, are treated as objects to be used and manipulated. Palestinian refugees seem to have become victims of political rape.

Yet something strange also happens to the soul of the oppressor where the dynamics of illegitimate power and deception become a hallmark of its hegemony. The sociologists Charles Derber[8] reminds us of the notion that hegemony, as articulated by the Italian social theorist Antonio Gramsci, is "power dressed up in universal values, such as freedom and prosperity." Derber goes on to argue that "Hegemons increasingly turn to military force when their military power and legitimacy begin to wane." Moreover, Fyodor Dostoyevsky's[9] Grand Inquisitor points out in *The Brothers Karamasov*:

> . . . we care for the weak too. They are sinful and rebellious, but in the end they too will become obedient. They will marvel at us and look on us as gods, because we are ready to endure the freedom which they have found so dreadful and to rule over them—so awful it will seem to them to be free. But we shall tell them that we are Thy servants and rule them in Thy name. We shall deceive them again . . . That deception will be our suffering, for we shall be forced to lie.

NOTES

1. Dan W. Dodson, *Power Conflict & Community Organizations* (New York: Council for American Unity, 1967), 7.

2. Samah Jabr, "The Struggle to Develop Identity While Under Occupation," *The Washington Report on Middle East Affairs* (December 2007): 19-20.

3. Mr. DuBois argues that: "It is a peculiar sensation, this double-consciousness, this sense of always looking at one's self through the eyes of others, of measuring one's soul by the tape of a world that looks on in amused contempt and pity." W.E.B. DuBois. *The Souls of Black Folk*. (Chicago: A.C. McClurg & Co., 1903); (Whitefish, MT: Kessinger Publishing, 2004), 3.

4. The Palestinian refugee infant mortality rate in Jordan in 2000, according to UNRWA, was 32 per 1000 live births. This rate is considered one of the highest in the region. See http://www.un.org/unrwa/publications/pdf/figures.pdf (26 August 2008).

5. Susan C. M. Scrimshaw, "Infant Mortality and Behavior in the Regulation of Family Size," *Population and Development Review*, 4, no. 3 (Sep. 1978): 383-403.

6. Deir Yassin is a small Palestinian village of about 750 residents located in the western outskirts of Jerusalem. The massacre was carried out by Jewish organizations, Haganah and Stern, headed by Menachem Begin who later became a prime minister of Israel. More than 250 Palestinians were killed on the morning of April 9, 1948. See: www.deiryassin.org (June 6, 2008); Ilan Pappe, *The Ethnic Cleansing of Palestine*. (Oxford, UK: Oneworld Publications, 2006), 90-91.

7. The term "human warehouses" used by the U.S. Committee for Refugees and refers to all refugee camps worldwide. http://www.refugees.org/uploadedFiles/Investigate/Anti_Warehousing/statement.pdf (19-Jan-2009).

8. Charles Derber, *The Wilding of America*. (New York: Worth Publishers), 112-113.

9. Fyodor Dostoyevsky, *The Brothers Karamazov*. Constance Garnett, tr. (New York: Barnes & Noble Classics, 2004), 235.

Epilogue

Studying social problems, domestic or international, poses a challenge to researchers. It is a point of tension between the scholar, on one hand, and the activist, on the other. What is a scholar's role in the face of oppression and injustice? Can one maintain neutrality? Can one uphold "objectivity" in the Weberian sense that sociologists are teachers—and not preachers? Or shall one take the Marxist view: "Enough with analysis, it is time for action"? Between these two extremes sociologists may find themselves maneuvering their research. The closer they get to the issues and to those who suffer as a result of them, the more engaged they find themselves.

Field observation as a research method intensifies such tensions. From this perspective, sociology becomes a window from which to view humanity. Researchers are placed in the midst of the story. We observe, we discuss, we ask questions, we reflect, and we challenge. The extensive work of Eliot Liebow[1] demonstrates that field observation engages researchers, empowers their research subjects and brings out the humanity of their narrative. This is how we gain new insights into the reality of the voiceless and invisible. Thus, researchers stand at the intersection of emotion and rationality. It is through such interactions, reflections and experiences that our understanding of the human story is illuminated—and that the invisible becomes visible.

This context presents serious questions for scholars: Have we done good work? And what makes a good work anyway? Because the research tools available to field researchers are based on our training and our personality, how can we judge the quality of our observations?

This project has been no exception. At times I was called upon to give my opinion and to take a stand on the Palestinian-Israeli conflict, on U.S. foreign policy, on the Palestinian right of return, and much more. There were times I wondered about the effectiveness of research in this area. After all, the

Palestinian *Al-Nakba* has now been around for more than sixty years. Why, then, should this project make any difference? Above all, I pondered on many occasions whether the voice of "invisible," oppressed poor people can truly be heard. Or, does this project make the invisible, in the words of Ralph Ellison, "un-visible"?

When research on social problems is carried out for the sake of knowledge and the benefit of humanity—something I have attempted to do in this study—it is easy to take a stand on issues of oppression and identity and make moral judgments about the underlying power relations. But the sociologist in me must also ask, in the tradition of functional analyses of Robert Merton[2] and Herbert Gans,[3] a different set of questions: What are the functions of this Palestinian tragedy? And who are the beneficiaries? Though deeply unsettling, these questions remain open for future research.

Instead, it is important to recall that in the midst of all these conflicting interactions, the stateless refugees continue to claim their self-respect. As one camp resident put it, "We may be poor and hungry, but we still have our dignity." Thus, if there is a lesson to be learned from my interactions with them, it is that humanity—kindness, compassion, determination, and dignity— really matters. The Palestinian refugees I encountered had lost so much, but they were also generous with their love, time, and hospitality. They opened their doors and their hearts to me. It is precisely as a result of their humanity that I have been challenged socially and intellectually—and I have become a better human being and a better sociologist. Although I have tried to lean closer to the scholar's side, I am very much aware that scholars also have a responsibility in bringing social issues to public consciousness. Public awareness is the beginning of social change; and it is in this sense that knowledge is indeed power. And there is more. As the philosopher and educators, Paulo Freire[4] reminds us that the oppressor "cannot find in this power the strength to liberate either the oppressed or themselves. Only power that springs from the weakness of the oppressed will be sufficiently strong to free both."

This research journey was undoubtedly one of the most difficult I have ever undertaken. I witnessed the misery, the despair, and the open national wound. The trauma remains vivid in the mind of the refugees, and the longer it remains untreated, the more dismal the conditions on the ground will be. Although this research was not about finding solutions, some may ask: So what? Why should we care? And what can be done about this tragedy? The questions could be numerous, the answers, lengthy, with the debate lingering as long as the *Nakba* has lasted and even beyond.

Assuming, however, that the parties, particularly holders of power, are truly interested in finding a peaceful and just solution, this research makes obvious two recommendations. One facet points to the daily social and personal reality on the ground: Invest in the human capital and implement necessary measures for the social and economic advancement of the refugees. Education, healthcare, housing, and employment are essential ingredients for giving people hope. Improving the daily reality on the ground is important but insufficient. Hence the second obvious and indispensable dimension: A political solution is badly needed, and the sooner the better. Again, assuming that a just peace is on the agenda of both sides, both have to recognize the humanity of the other and take important steps in that direction. On the Palestinian side, I am still waiting for the "Palestinian Gandhi" to emerge. It seems to me that when groups or nations resort to violence, they might end up losing their soul. As to Western countries and Israel, it is important to recognize the fact that they have never acknowledged their role in the *Nakba* or thereafter. For those who wonder where to begin, an official public apology to the Palestinians is a good starting point. Sincere apologies have the power to heal and the power to transform reality; they set the stage for reconciliation; and above all, they have the power to humanize the Other—they make them visible.

NOTES

1. Eliot Liebow, *Tally's Corner: A Study of Negro Streetcorner Men* (Boston: Little, Brown, 1967) and *Tell Them Who I Am: The Lives of Homeless Women* (New York: The Free Press, 1993).

2. Robert K. Merton, *Social Theory and Social Structure* (New York: The Free Press, 1957).

3. Herbert Gans, "The Uses of Poverty: The Poor Pay All." *Social Policy*, (July/August, 1971): 20-24.

4. Paulo Freire. Pedagogy of the Oppressed. (New York: Continuum Publishing, 1970) 28.

Index

About the Author

Nabil Marshood is a professor of sociology at Hudson County Community College in New Jersey, where he teaches courses in race and ethnic relations, sociology of religion, sociology of the family, and general sociology. Prior to his academic career, Dr. Marshood was a practicing clinician in the fields of rehabilitation and mental health. He received his BA and MA degrees from the Hebrew University in Jerusalem, and his doctorate from Columbia University School of Social Work. Nabil is a recipient of a Mid-Career Fellowship from Princeton University, with concentration on social theory and sociology of religion; a Fulbright Fellowship; and a number of grants offering community education about peace and conflict resolution, and religious pluralism. In addition to writing articles on higher education in community colleges and religious pluralism, he is the author of *Palestinian Teenage Immigrants and Refugees Speak Out*, published by Rosen Publishing Group, and a coauthor of *Everyday Sociology,* a sociology textbook published by StarPoint Press. Nabil is fluent in English, Arabic, and Hebrew.

25488903R00082

Made in the USA
Middletown, DE
31 October 2015